# TALES AND TRAVELS

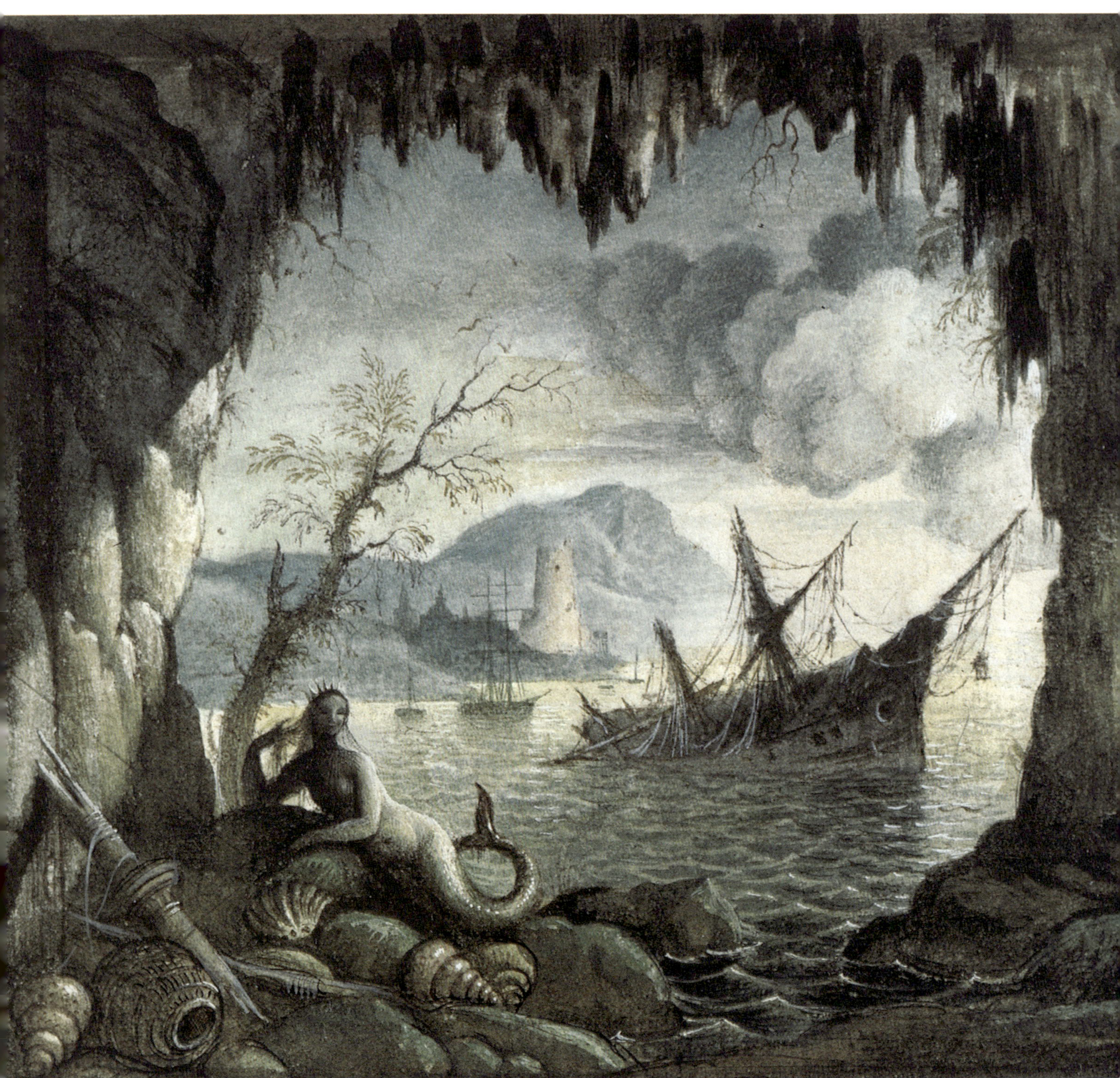

# TALES AND TRAVELS

## *Drawings Recently Acquired on the Sunny Crawford von Bülow Fund*

KATHLEEN STUART

*With contributions by*

Jennifer Tonkovich and Andaleeb Badiee Banta

Foreword by Charles E. Pierce, Jr.

THE MORGAN LIBRARY & MUSEUM, NEW YORK

Exhibition at The Morgan Library & Museum,
29 June–23 September 2007

This catalogue was made possible by the Andrew W. Mellon Research and Publications Fund.

LIBRARY OF CONGRESS CATALOGING-IN-PUBLICATION DATA
Pierpont Morgan Library.
Tales and travels : drawings recently acquired on the Sunny Crawford von Bülow Fund / Kathleen Stuart ; with contributions by Jennifer Tonkovich and Andaleeb Banta ; foreword by Charles E. Pierce, Jr.
p. cm.
Catalog of an exhibition at the Morgan Library & Museum, June 29–Sept. 23, 2007.
Includes bibliographical references and index.
ISBN 978-0-87598-146-8 (alk. paper)
1. Drawing, European—Exhibitions. 2. Drawing—New York (State)—New York—Exhibitions. 3. Pierpont Morgan Library—Exhibitions. 4. Von Bülow, Martha Crawford, 1931—Art collections—Exhibitions. I. Stuart, Kathleen. II. Tonkovich, Jennifer. III. Banta, Andaleeb. IV. Title.
NC225.P52 2007
741.94'0747471—dc22 2007018072



ISBN: 978-0-87598-146-8

Printed in the United States of America

*Note to the Reader*
In measurements, height precedes width. Works cited in published references are reproduced unless otherwise indicated.

The authors are grateful to the following individuals for their assistance with this catalogue: Laura Bennett, André Brutillot, Andrew Clayton-Payne, Dr. Peter Fuhring, Prof. Jerome de la Gorce, Armin Kunz, Briony Llewellyn, Kim Sloane, Peter Styra, and Caroline Williams.

Published by The Morgan Library & Museum
Karen Banks, Publications Manager
Patricia Emerson, Senior Editor
Elizabeth Moore, Editorial Assistant

*Project staff*
Marilyn Palmeri, Manager, Photography and Rights
Eva Soos, Assistant Manager, Photography and Rights

Designed by Bessas & Ackerman
Color consulting by Sally Fisher
Printed and bound by Thames Printing Company, Norwich, CT

FRONT COVER: Francis Danby, *The Procession of Cristna* (No. 26)

FRONTISPIECE: Rex Whistler, *The Mermaid: Design for a Cave Room Mural* (No. 37)

*Contents*

# *Director's Foreword*

We are extremely pleased to present *Tales and Travels: Drawings Recently Acquired on the Sunny Crawford von Bülow Fund*. This is the second catalogue of drawings purchased for the Morgan with funds provided by the family of Sunny Crawford von Bülow. In 1995 the Morgan first celebrated works acquired on the fund since the late 1970s with an exhibition and catalogue titled *Fantasy and Reality: Drawings from the Sunny Crawford von Bülow Collection*. Since the first gift in 1977—the insightful *Portrait of Charles-Désiré Norry (1796–1818)* by Jean-Auguste-Dominique Ingres—Sunny, and more recently her daughter Cosima Pavoncelli, made important acquisitions for the department of Drawings and Prints. During these three decades, they have added eighty-two drawings and an album of sixty-four sheets to the collection. The publication of the present catalogue honors the memory of Sunny von Bülow and her enduring and profoundly generous commitment to the Morgan.

The selections for the Morgan were guided by a taste largely for eighteenth-century drawings and watercolors encompassing both rococo and neoclassical traditions. The group presented in 1995 displayed an affinity for works by French artists and featured brilliant examples by such masters as Antoine Watteau, Ingres, and François Boucher. More recently, Cosima's taste has turned toward works by British artists. Among the many important new acquisitions are a superb black-chalk view of Rome by Richard Wilson, commissioned in Italy in about 1752 by the 2nd Earl of Dartmouth, and the evocative *Procession of Cristna*, a delicate watercolor on vellum by the Irish-born artist Francis Danby, which is reproduced on the cover of the present catalogue.

The chronological range of works acquired on the von Bülow fund has expanded in recent years. The drawings presented here span three centuries and include several European schools. The earliest, dated 1613, is by the sixteenth-century Flemish artist Jacob Hoefnagel—*Orpheus Charming the Animals*, a meticulously drawn work in watercolor and gouache on vellum. The newest drawing, dated 1929, is by the early-twentieth-century British artist and designer Rex Whistler—a delightful watercolor entitled *The Mermaid*. In between are landscapes both familiar and foreign by the nineteenth-century artists John Sell Cotman and David Roberts, drawings of allegorical subjects and those illustrating literary themes by such masters as the seventeenth-century artist Willem van Mieris and by contemporaries of William Blake, namely John Mortimer and Edward Westall. Also represented are nature and figure studies made in exotic locales by Maria Sybilla Merian, Louis-Nicolas de Lespinasse, and Eugène Delacroix, as well as designs for decorative projects by French artists Gilles-Paul Cauvet and Jean I Berain. Despite this broad range, the group is particularly cohesive, and the drawings are highly finished. Many were made as independent works of art.

Coinciding with the publication of the present catalogue, the Morgan has mounted an exhibition of the entire von Bülow collection to commemorate the tremendous significance of the fund to the continued growth of its holdings. I am thankful to Kathleen Stuart, Assistant Curator of Drawings and Prints, who has created a beautiful catalogue that fully discusses each new acquisition since 1995. Ms. Stuart was ably assisted by her colleagues in the department of Drawings and Prints, Jennifer Tonkovich and Andaleeb Badiee Banta. This volume was thoughtfully edited by Patricia Emerson, and the splendid photography of the works is indebted to Joseph Zehavi and Marilyn Palmeri. I also thank Cara Dufour Denison for supervising the installation of the exhibition, and Rhoda Eitel-Porter, Charles W. Engelhard Curator and Head of the Department of Drawings and Prints, for overseeing the entire project.

The drawings documented herein comprise an exceptional group of thirty-seven sheets assembled in just over a decade and represent an ongoing commitment of extraordinary generosity for which we remain deeply grateful.

Charles E. Pierce, Jr.

JACOB HOEFNAGEL Flemish, Antwerp 1575–ca. 1630 Holland?

# 1. *Orpheus Charming the Animals,* 1613

Watercolor and gouache, heightened with white gouache, over traces of black chalk, on vellum mounted to panel; bordered in gold. 6 9/16 × 8 5/16 inches (167 × 211 mm).

Signed and dated at lower left, in gold, *Ja: Houfnagl / 1613.*

PROVENANCE: Private collection, Cornwall, England; acquired from Artemis SA, Luxembourg.

BIBLIOGRAPHY: *Artemis* 2000, no. 4.

EXHIBITIONS: New York 2003, no. 12; New York 2006, no. 35.

1998.22

Jacob Hoefnagel served as court painter to Rudolf II in Prague (r. 1576–1612) from 1602 until 1613, succeeding his father, the miniaturist Joris Hoefnagel (1542–1601). Jacob's specialty, in accordance with the emperor's taste, was small-format mythological scenes on vellum or copper (Vignau-Wilberg 1994, p. 26). The present drawing is such a work, and its date and exquisite finish suggest that it may have been a courtly commission. It represents the Greek god Orpheus playing music for an assemblage of animals in a verdant landscape. The subject was frequently represented in northern European art in the late sixteenth and early seventeenth centuries because it reflected the vogue for encyclopedic representations of nature.

Several animals in this drawing—the buck, the dog reclining at the feet of Orpheus, the lion, and the leopard and fox—are identical to those in a painting by Frans Pourbus I (1545/46–1581), *Orpheus Among the Animals,* signed and dated 1570, in the Palazzo Pitti, Florence (Chiarini and Padovani 2003, vol. 2, p. 304, no. 494). The fox also appears in identical form in a manuscript illuminated by Joris Hoefnagel in 1591–94, Georg Bocskay's *Schriftmusterbuch* in the Kunsthistorisches Museum, Vienna (fol. 102; Vignau-Wilberg 1969, vol. 2, pl. 64). This suggests that both the Pourbus painting and the present drawing may derive from a lost common model by Joris Hoefnagel. Alternatively, the elder Hoefnagel may have provided additional sources for the present drawing, a proposal supported by the close correspondence between several other drawings or paintings by the elder Hoefnagel and representations of animals in the present sheet; see, for example, the ox in the drawing *View of Ambras* in the Kunsthistorisches Museum at Schloss Ambras, Austria (Vignau-Wilberg 1969, vol. 2, pl. 93), the ostrich in the manuscript *The Four Elements* in the National Gallery of Art, Washington, D.C. (vol. 4, pl. 1; Maselis et al. 1999, fig. 70), and the monkey in Jacob's book of engravings after his father's designs, *Archetypa studiaque patris Georgii Hoefnagelii,* published in Frankfurt in 1592 (title page of part 1; Vignau-Wilberg 1994, pl. 125). Pourbus's portrait of the Hoefnagel family of about 1581, in the Musées royaux des Beaux-Arts de Belgique, Brussels, documents his close relationship with the elder Hoefnagel (Brussels 1957, no. 944, pl. 30).

The present drawing appears to have been the model for the painting attributed to Jan Brueghel the Younger (1601–1678) in the Prado, Madrid, *Orpheus and the Animals,* the foreground of which copies the Morgan drawing in almost every detail (Díaz Padrón 1995, vol. 1, no. 1413).

As Lee Hendrix observed, the landscape of the present drawing, especially the rocky outcroppings, gnarled roots, and fir trees, is strongly reminiscent of the work of Roelandt Savery (1576–1639), who was resident in Prague in 1603–13 and whose landscape style was widely influential among Rudolf II's court artists (communication with the author, 24 February 2005).

KS

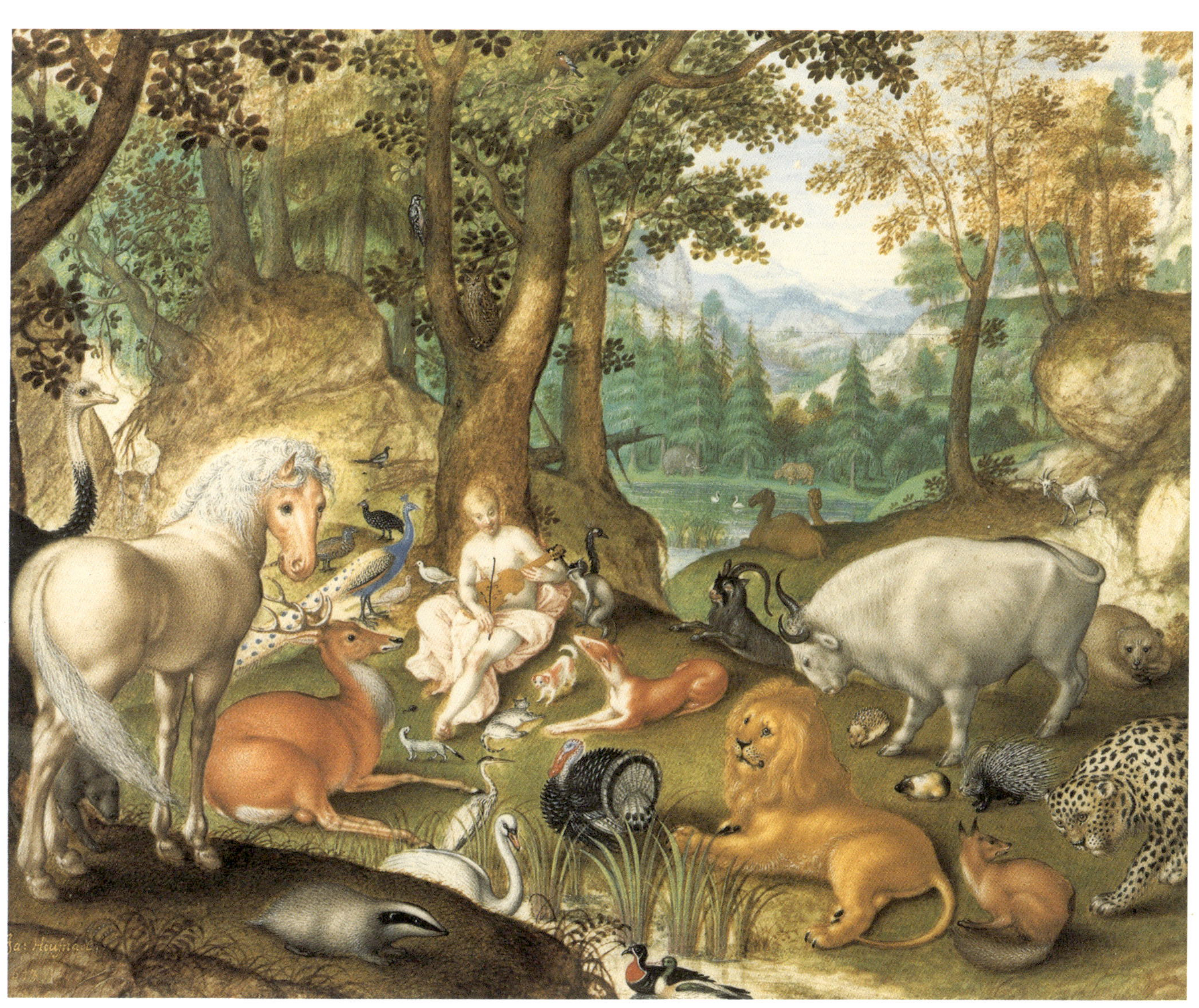

# 2. *Black Tegu Lizard* (Tupinambis teguixin)

Pen and black ink, watercolor and gouache, gum arabic, heightened with white gouache, on vellum; framing line in black chalk. 13 × 17 inches (329 × 430 mm).

Inscribed on verso, along left edge, in the hand of van der Marck Ægzn, in graphite, *N.100 uit Boek f. van Jan Bisschop's Verk. te Rottm. Juni 1771 / 44- / Een Surinaamsche Sauvegard, door Maria Sybilla Merian.*

PROVENANCE: Jan Bisschop (1680/81–1771), Rotterdam; his sale, Bosch and Arrenberg, Rotterdam, 24 June 1771, Album A, lot 100; Johan van der Marck Ægzn (1707–1772), Leiden (Lugt 3001); his sale, de Winter & IJver, Amsterdam, 29ff. November 1773, Album H, lot 717; Dr. Jan Tak (1729–1780), Leiden; his sale, Jan van de Vinne, Haarlem, 10–11 October 1780, Album B, lot 170; Jonkheer Lodewijk J. Quarles van Ufford (1719–1781), The Hague; his sale, van Pappelendam, Haarlem, 23–24 March 1784, Album 4, lot 174; sale, Sotheby's, London, 7 July 1999, lot 37; acquired from Thomas Williams Fine Art, Ltd., London.

BIBLIOGRAPHY: New York 2000, no. 24; New York 2003, no. 21; Turner 2006, no. 154.

EXHIBITION: New York 2003, no. 21.

2001.10

A gifted artist who trained with her stepfather, the flower painter Jacob Marrell (1614–1681), Merian developed an early interest in insects and their transformations, or metamorphoses. In 1699 she embarked on a two-year expedition to the Dutch colony of Surinam in South America to observe and make drawings of its insects, plants, and animals. On her return to Amsterdam in 1701 (owing to illness), Merian began working up the life drawings she had made on her expedition into large, finished watercolors on vellum. These served as the *modelli* for the engravings in her monumental publication *Metamorphosis insectorum Surinamensium* (Amsterdam, 1705), which comprised sixty engravings of insects and plants indigenous to Surinam. A serious scholar, Merian was in close touch with the leading scientists of the day, and each print in the *Metamorphosis* is accompanied by a detailed commentary in Latin by Caspar Commelin (ca. 1667–1731), then director of the Amsterdam Botanical Gardens.

Merian returned to Amsterdam with drawings not only of flowers, plants, and insects but also of reptiles and other fauna, intending to produce a second volume devoted to these animals. Although her plans were not realized, after her death her daughter Johanna Herolt published a second edition of the *Metamorphosis* (1719) with twelve plates of illustrations of reptiles and amphibians, including this subject. The present watercolor is the preparatory *modello,* in reverse, for plate 70 of this second edition. Merian's talents for descriptive naturalism are brilliantly evident in this work. With meticulous care she recorded the texture of the lizard's skin, using both the pen and the brush to model form and suggest the animal's sinuous physicality. The lizard's pose is conventional and intended to show all four feet. In the plate, which Merian may have engraved herself, the addition of a rocky landscape setting makes the uplifted hind leg intelligible.

Although traditionally entitled the *Sauvegarde of Jacruarú,* the type of New World monitor lizard represented here is commonly known as a black or blue tegu (*Tupinambis teguixin* of the family Teiidae). Merian's illustration represents an adult lizard, probably male, that grows to almost three feet in length. Its range extends from northern South America to central Brazil. While not officially endangered, tegus are hunted assiduously for their skin. On plate 4 of the *Metamorphosis,* Merian depicted a smaller example of the same type of lizard climbing the stem of a branch of manioc (see Haarlem 1998, no. 127).

Among the other known *modelli* for the *Metamorphosis* is *A Crocodile Fighting with a Snake,* for plate 69, in the Royal Library at Windsor Castle (see Rücker and Stearn 1982, p. 21).

KS

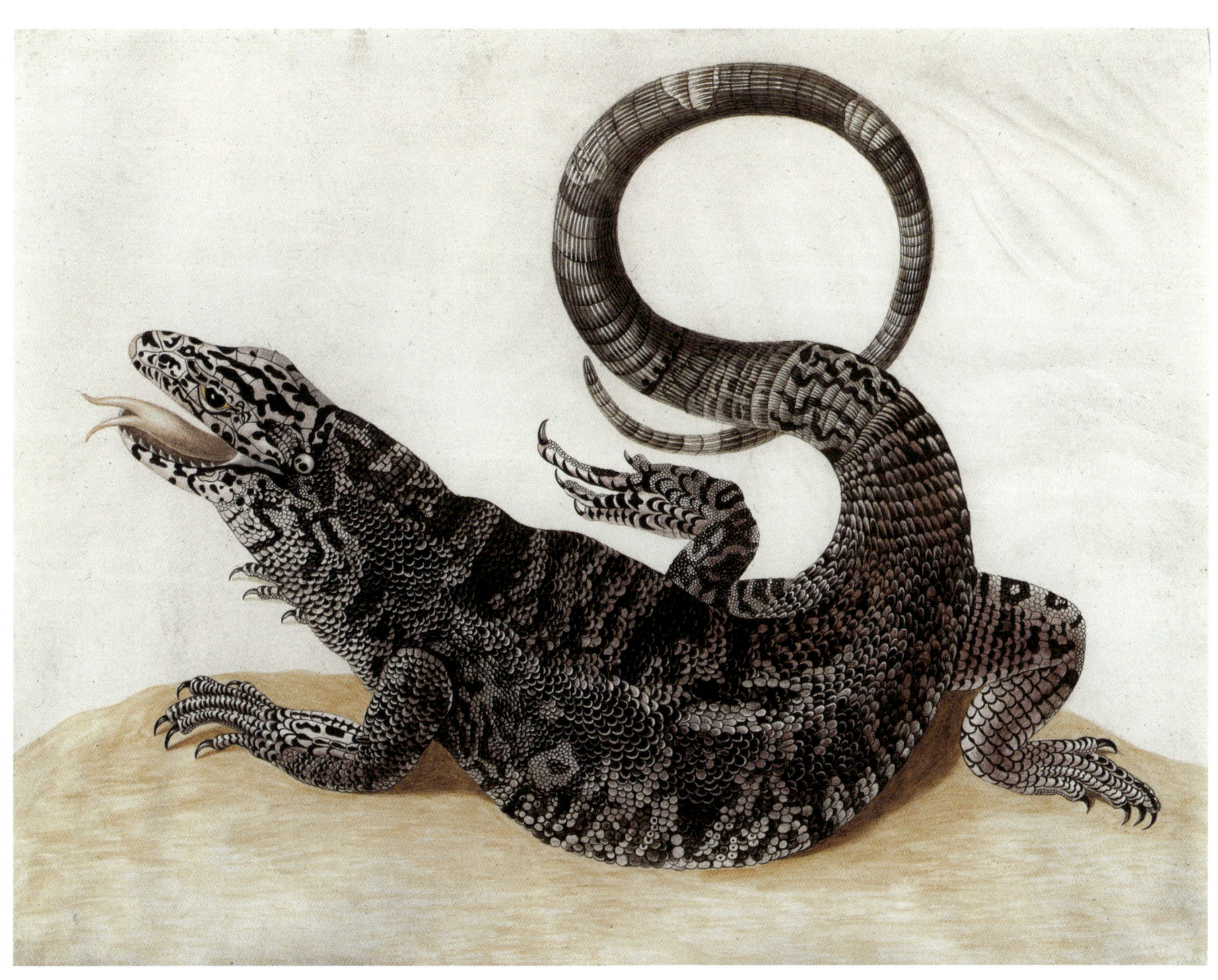

WILLEM VAN MIERIS Dutch, Leiden 1662–1747 Leiden

# 3. *Joseph and Potiphar's Wife* (Genesis 39:11–12), ca. 1691–96

Gouache on vellum; framing line in black ink. 6¾ × 5⅝ inches (171 × 144 mm).

Signed and dated at upper right, in black ink, *W. van Mieris Fecit Anñ 1693*. Inscribed on old mount, below drawing, in brown ink, *—Joseph tempted by Potiphars wife— / Genesis. Chap.xxxix = ver^s 11 & 12*; signature and date inscribed on separate piece of card, in same hand as previous inscription, now attached to backboard, in brown ink, *W.v. Mieris Fecit Anno 1693*.

PROVENANCE: Probably Jonas Witsen II (1676–1715), Amsterdam; his grandson, Jonas Witsen IV (1733–1788), Amsterdam; his sale, Terwen . . . de Bosch, Amsterdam, 16 August 1790, Album B, lot 40; Jan de Groot (1733–1801), The Hague and Amsterdam; his sale, van der Schley, Amsterdam, 10 December 1804, Album E, lot 17; C. S. Roos, Amsterdam; Gerard van Nijmegen (1735–1808), Rotterdam; his sale, van der Schley . . . de Vries, Amsterdam, 20ff. March 1809, Album F, lot 32; Hendrik van Eyl Sluyter (1739–1814), Amsterdam; his sale, van der Schley . . . de Vries, Amsterdam, 26 September 1814, Album D, lot 20; C. J. Nieuwenhuys (1799–1883), Brussels and Oxford Lodge, Wimbledon; private collection, France; acquired from Bob P. Haboldt & Co., New York and Paris.

BIBLIOGRAPHY: Elen 1995, no. 2; Turner 2006, no. 399.

EXHIBITIONS: New York 2001–2, one of a pair in no. 59; New York 2006a, no. 32.

2001.46

Willem van Mieris was the son and pupil of Frans van Mieris (1635–1681), one of the Netherlands' best-known *fijnschilders,* or "fine painters," who specialized in meticulously rendered, highly decorative paintings featuring trompe l'oeil representations of textures. The younger van Mieris carried on his father's tradition, producing paintings and drawings in watercolor and gouache for discriminating collectors. Although the majority of his oeuvre comprised genre pictures in the tradition of the "fine painters," Willem van Mieris concentrated to a greater extent than his father on allegorical subjects and themes from classical literature.

Executed in a miniaturist technique using tiny, stippled dots of gouache on vellum, the present drawing belongs to a series of twenty small but highly finished works that van Mieris made between 1691 and 1696. Albert Elen (1995) has suggested that the series may have been commissioned from van Mieris by Jonas Witsen II (1676–1715), a young member of the Amsterdam city government and director of the local *kunstkamer* (chamber of arts). The whereabouts of half the drawings are known, with examples in public collections, such as the Rijksprentenkabinet, Amsterdam, the Prentenkabinet der Universiteit, Leiden, the British Museum, London, and the Boijmans Van Beuningen Museum, Rotterdam.

The drawing represents a scene from the Old Testament story of Potiphar, captain of the Pharoah's guard, and his household slave Joseph. In the scene depicted here, Potiphar's wife tries to seduce Joseph, who pulls away and attempts to flee from her advances. Although the subject was popular among artists of the sixteenth and seventeenth centuries, who typically represented the dramatic scene shown here, van Mieris may have found inspiration for the pose of Potiphar's wife in the figure of Venus in Rubens's *Venus and Adonis* (Metropolitan Museum of Art, New York; Baetjer 1995, p. 279), who faces the viewer, gestures dramatically, and is nude but for a swath of fabric draped across one leg.

The present gouache employs compositional devices used in van Mieris's oil paintings of the 1680s and 1690s. Historical subjects are set against a background with elements of classical architecture and ornament. Such scenes, as is the case here, usually feature classical bas-reliefs and sculpture set in niches, draped bed curtains that close off one side of the composition, and a column that acts as a *repoussoir* device. Comparable examples include the signed and dated painting of 1685 of the same subject in the Niedersächsisches Landesmuseum, Hannover (see Amsterdam 1989, no. 21), and a painting of 1691 in the Wallace Collection, London (see Ingamells 1992, pp. 216–17).

KS

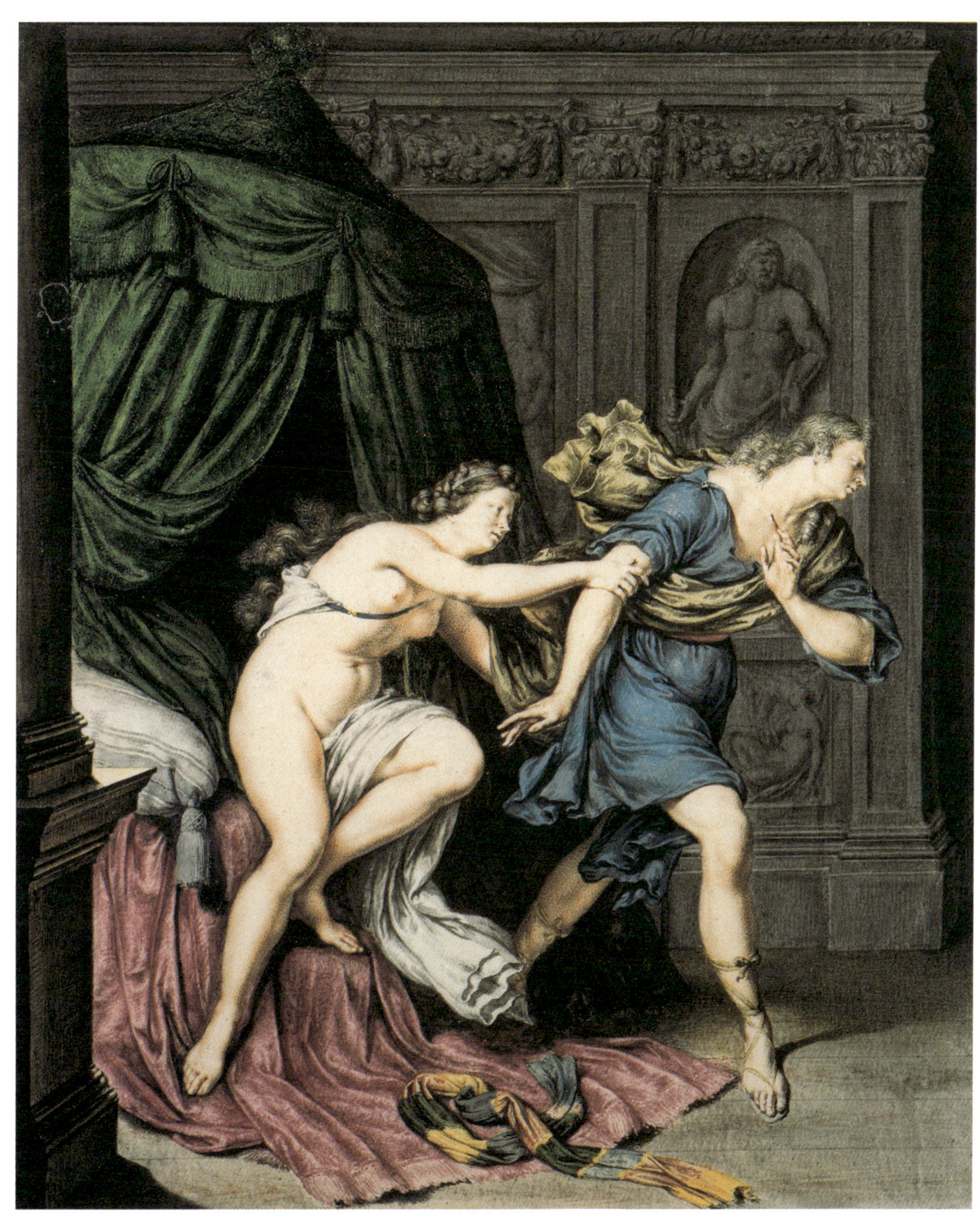

# 4. *Design with Apollo on His Chariot Smiting the Python*

Pen and black ink, gray wash, over black chalk; the nymph at left center drawn on a separate sheet and pasted in; verso rubbed with red chalk and outlines incised for transfer. 10⅜ × 13 inches (262 × 329 mm).

PROVENANCE: Paul Ratouis de Limay (b. 1881); sale, Paris, Renaud, 19 December 2001, lot 7, repr.; acquired from C. G. Boerner, Inc., New York.

BIBLIOGRAPHY: Weigert 1937, under no. 60.

EXHIBITIONS: Aix-en-Provence 1954, no. 26; Nancy 1961, no. 55; New York 2003a, no. 27.

2003.11

Berain served as *dessinateur du cabinet du roi* (draftsman to the king) under Louis XIV from 1674 until his death and achieved great fame as a designer for the Paris Opéra and for the royal *menus plaisirs* (king's entertainments). His innovative decorative projects provided a model that was to have a lasting influence on the *ornemanistes* of the eighteenth century. The present design depicts Apollo with his bow and lyre emerging from his chariot. He tramples on Python, the serpent guarding the oracle at Pytho (later Delphi), which he slew with his bow and arrow. The god is flanked by two pairs of herms representing the seasons; between each pair stands a smoking tripod, a reference to Apollo's prophetic powers. A device consisting of Apollo's lyre and quiver surmounts the cornice above each pair of herms. Above the crown atop the central niche are representations of the signs of the zodiac.

This design was long known only through an unsigned print in Jacques Thuret's 1711 publication of the artist's engraved works (pl. 77); Thuret added the inscription *I Berain delin.* (designed by Jean Berain). Roger-Armand Weigert, the first modern scholar to catalogue Berain's oeuvre, considered that the drawing undeniably served as preparation for the print, although, lacking comparative material, he had reservations as to whether the drawing was by Berain or by the unknown artist who produced the engraving (Weigert 1937, vol. 2, p. 64). Peter Fuhring, who recognizes the sheet as Berain's original design, suggested that Weigert's reservations likely stemmed from the irregular appearance of the pen line, which was damaged when the design was traced with a stylus for transfer to the copperplate. Berain certainly used the sheet as a working drawing. The winged female restraining the horse at left is drawn on a patch pasted to the drawing, undoubtedly correcting what lies beneath. The Apollonian scenes embellishing the roundels between the herms and the relief panels on the front of the plinth found in the print have not yet been added.

In his *Notes manuscrits* in the Bibliothèque Nationale de France, the eighteenth-century connoisseur Pierre-Jean Mariette described the composition as a tapestry design. Berain is thought to have made designs for more than 250 tapestries for the royal tapestry works at Beauvais. His designs were also used outside France. The present composition was woven in Erlangen between 1734 and 1740 by Jean Dechasaux the younger, son of a Protestant weaver from Aubusson. The tapestry, in the Bayerisches Nationalmuseum, Munich (inv. no. 93/589), deviates in several details from the drawing and the overall design has been cropped and compressed into a narrower rectangle. Woven after Berain's death, the tapestry is an example of the continued reliance—that lasted well into the eighteenth century—on such designs as the present one.

JT

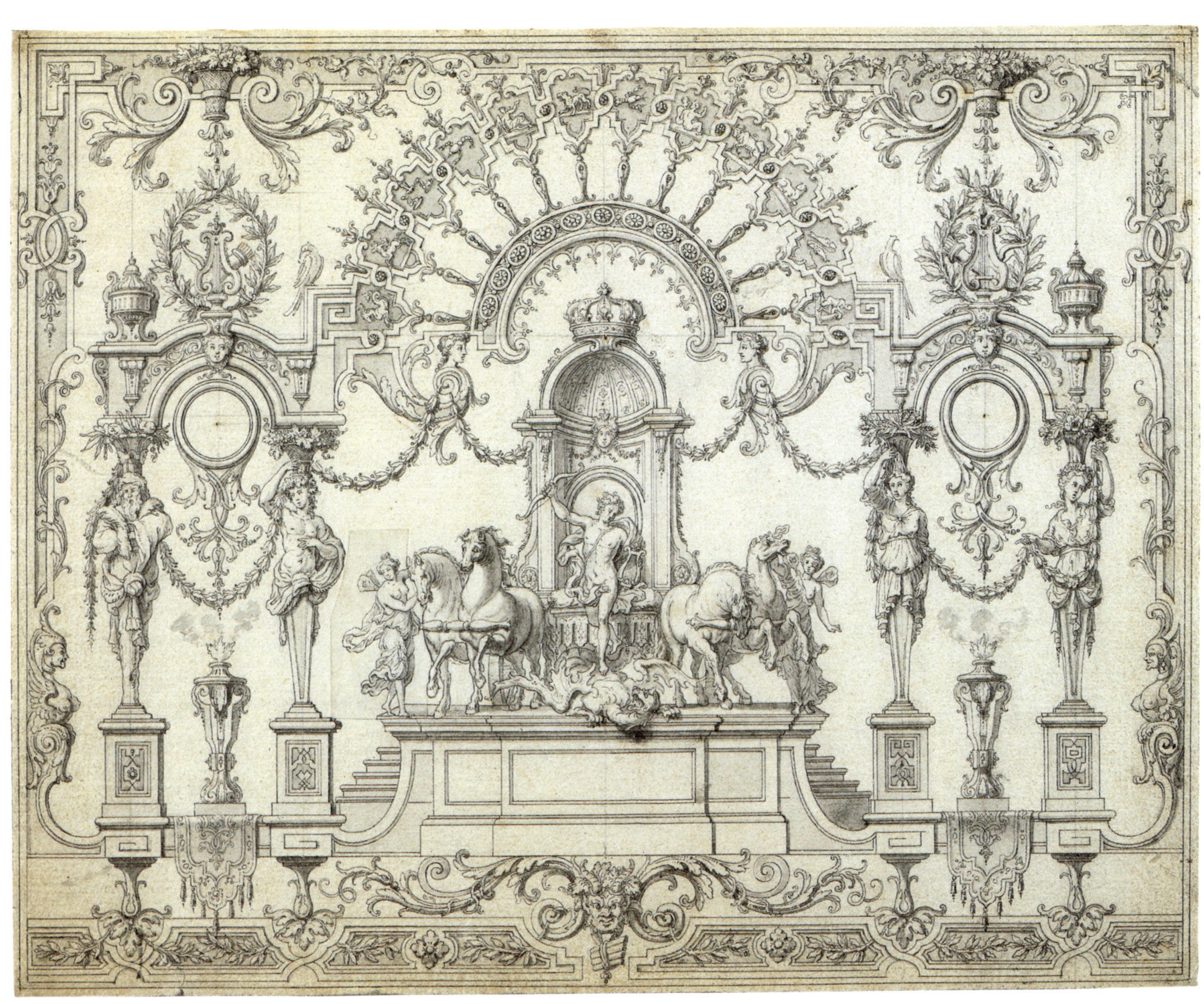

GILLES PAUL CAUVET French, Aix-en-Provence 1731–1788 Paris

# 5. *Cherub Gardeners* (Les amours jardiniers), ca. 1771–1777

Red chalk, with traces of black chalk in figures of putti; framing line in red chalk. 18¾ × 6<sup>13</sup>⁄<sub>16</sub> inches (475 × 171 mm).

PROVENANCE: Martine-Marie-Pol, Comtesse de Béhague (1870–1939), Paris; sale, Paris, Hôtel Drouot, 29 November 1995, part of lot 107; acquired from Didier Aaron, Inc., New York.

EXHIBITION: Paris and New York [1996], no. 12.

1997.84

The second half of the eighteenth century was a period of sustained production and innovation in the decorative arts. Cauvet was one of the principal designers of architectural decoration inspired by the elegant paintings and objects recently discovered at Pompeii and Herculaneum. His style paid homage to the classical themes and symmetrical compositions of antiquity. Cauvet became director of the Académie de Saint-Luc in 1766 and was named sculptor to Monsieur (the king's brother and a count of Cauvet's native Provence) in 1774. He worked occasionally as an architect but was prolific as a designer of interior and exterior ornament for the grand hôtels of Paris.

The present sheet is related to Cauvet's self-published pattern book of ornamental prints, the *Recueil d'ornemans à l'usage des jeunes artistes qui se destinent à la décoration des bâtiments* (Collection of Ornamental Motifs for the Use of Young Artists Intending To Be Decorators of Buildings), 1777. As editor, Cauvet continued to add plates to the *recueil,* resulting in an extraordinary variety among extant copies. About one hundred drawings, engraved by various hands in the same direction as the drawings, are known. According to Mary Myers, Cauvet began making drawings for the series as early as 1771, with the first prints being produced by 1774 (Myers in Baltimore and elsewhere 1984–85, pp. 215–17). Cauvet's elegant design reveals the new taste for low-relief decorative elements in stucco or wood in place of the previous fashion for painted interior decoration. The present drawing was engraved by Jacques le Roy (1739–ca. 1789) for the *recueil.*

Cauvet's design retains the format of the rococo arabesque that was popularized much earlier by Antoine Watteau, though in a more symmetrical and orderly composition. At center, a trio of putti balances a basket of flowers atop a globe. The hunting horn and quiver above and the harvesting implements (rake, shovel, flail, and scythe) and grapes below suggest that the design may be for a panel representing autumn in a series of four seasons. Directly beneath the putti are a torch and another quiver, emblems of Amor, as are the doves flanking the scene. This lighthearted combination of love and rustic pleasures is characteristic of the themes that persisted into the neoclassical period.

JT

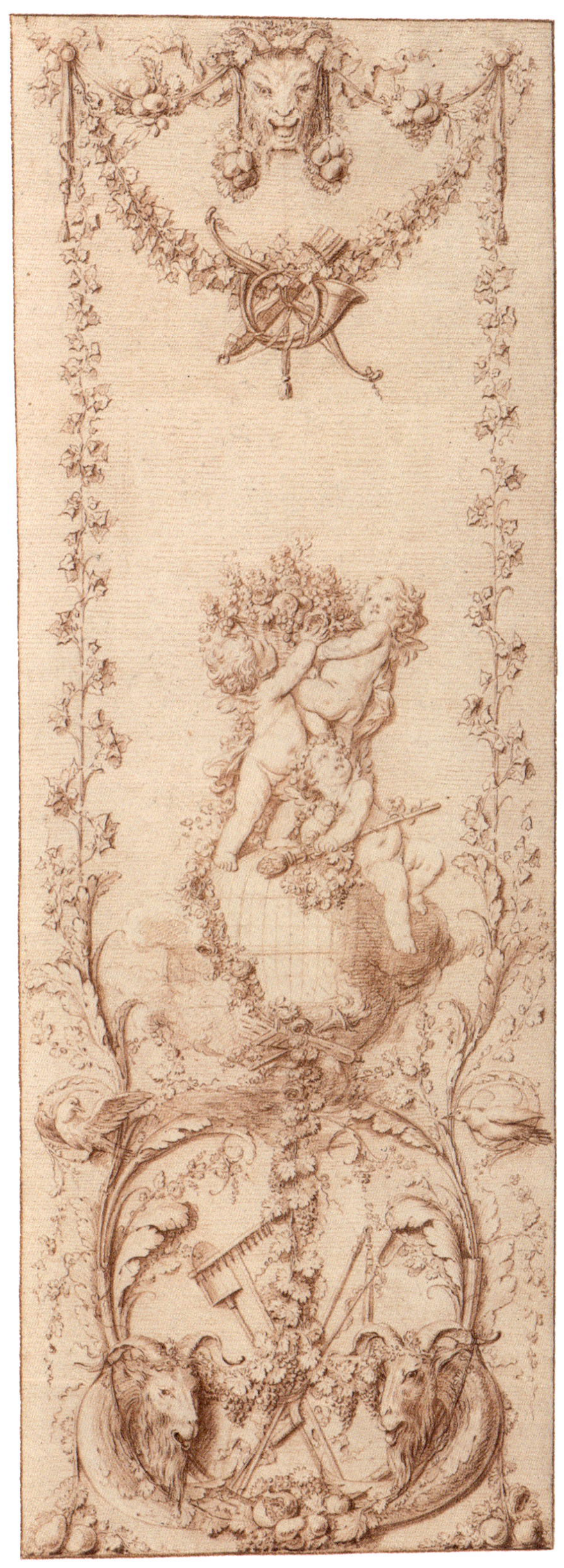

# 6. *The Presentation of an Ambassador to the Sultan in the Hall of Petitions of the Topkapi Palace, Constantinople,* 1790

Graphite, pen and brown ink, watercolor and gouache, heightened with white. 9⅞ × 15⅜ inches (252 × 392 mm).

Signed with the artist's initials and dated, *d. L. 1790.*

PROVENANCE: Sale, Stockholms Auktionsverk, Stockholm, 25 November 1997, part of lot 1293 (with No. 7); sale, Christie's, London, 7 July 1998, lot 237; sale, Christie's, New York, 22 January 2003, part of lot 70 (with No. 7); acquired from Andrew Clayton-Payne Ltd., London.

BIBLIOGRAPHY: Borne 1998, p. 42; Clayton-Payne 2007, pp. 74–77.

2006.2

Before becoming an artist, the talented but little-known Lespinasse had a military career, during which he earned membership in the royal order of St. Louis. It is perhaps from experience with topographical drawings that he came to develop a particular skill for panoramic city views and architectural interiors, both relying on depictions of vast, complex spaces, enlivened by many figures. In fact, at the end of his life he produced a treatise on perspective. Lespinasse had his public debut as an artist at age forty-four, when an engraving after one of his drawings appeared in the *Mercure de France.* He was accepted by the Académie royale in 1787 as a "painter of landscapes and perspective views in gouache" and then began to exhibit at the official Salon, which he would continue to do until 1801. His reputation was further established during this period by the ongoing publication of the *Voyage pittoresque de la France* (1784–92), containing his panoramic city scenes.

Lespinasse's gift for compositions with vast numbers of figures led to his involvement in Ignace Mouradja d'Ohsson's *Tableau général de l'Empire Othoman* (Portrait of the Ottoman Empire; Paris, Firmin Didot). The first two volumes appeared in 1787 and 1789, while the French Revolution delayed the publication of the third volume until 1824. Along with Moreau le jeune (No. 8), whose view of a Turkish interior was engraved for the same publication, Lespinasse and others developed carefully finished drawings preparatory for the plates. *The Presentation of an Ambassador* was engraved as the final plate in the third volume of d'Ohsson's publication in a chapter on the relations of the Ottoman court with foreign powers (*Audience d'un ministre européen;* vol. 3, 1824, pl. 233). *The Reception of an Ambassador* (No. 7) apparently was not used for the project.

Both scenes evince Lespinasse's skill. In the *Reception of an Ambassador,* the view of water suggests that the room depicted may be at the grand vizier's *yali* (mansion), which was located along the water with a view of the strait and served as his summer house. The grand vizier often entertained visiting dignitaries with a meal before their reception by the sultan at Topkapi Palace. The *Presentation of an Ambassador* is set at Topkapi Palace, the seat of the Ottoman sultan, in the grand *arz odasi* (Hall of Petitions) used for official receptions. The sultan sits on his elaborate divan, with the grand vizier and high admiral to his left. The ambassador wears a sable-trimmed robe, while the members of his entourage wear caftans; their wigs and hats reveal that they are probably French. Following the closely prescribed court protocol described in d'Ohsson's text, the ambassador and his entourage present their letters of credential to the court and a court translator conveys the ambassador's speech.

Many of the finished watercolor models by French artists for illustrations in the *Tableau général* were based on designs commissioned by d'Ohsson while still in Constantinople. In fact, a preliminary design executed in red chalk for *The Reception of an Ambassador,* now in a private collection, has been attributed to Jean-Baptiste van Mour (1671–1737), a French artist based in the capital (Christie's, New York, 22 January 2003, under no. 70). JT

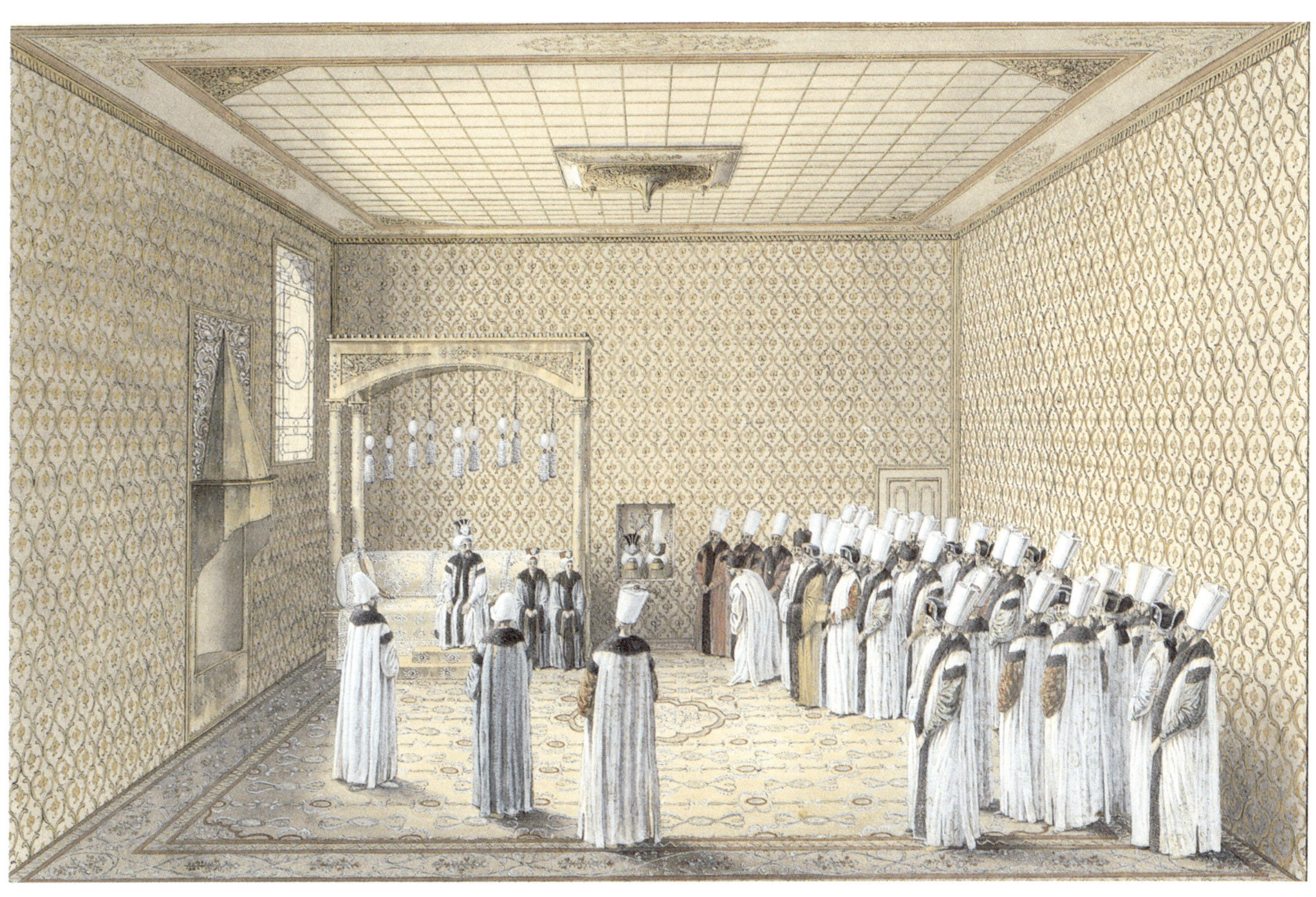

LOUIS-NICOLAS DE LESPINASSE French, Pouilly-sur-Loire 1734–1808 Paris

# 7. *The Reception of an Ambassador by the Grand Vizier at His* Yali *on the Shores of the Bosphorus*

Graphite, pen and brown ink, watercolor and gouache, heightened with white. 9⅞ × 15⅜ inches (252 × 392 mm).

Signed with the artist's initials and dated, *d. L. 1790.*

PROVENANCE: Sale, Stockholms Auktionsverk, Stockholm, 25 November 1997, part of lot 1293 (with No. 6); sale, Christie's, London, 7 July 1998, lot 236; sale, Christie's, New York, 22 January 2003, part of lot 70 (with No. 6); acquired from Andrew Clayton-Payne Ltd., London.

BIBLIOGRAPHY: Borne 1998, p. 42; Clayton-Payne 2007, pp. 74–77.

2006.3

See No. 6.

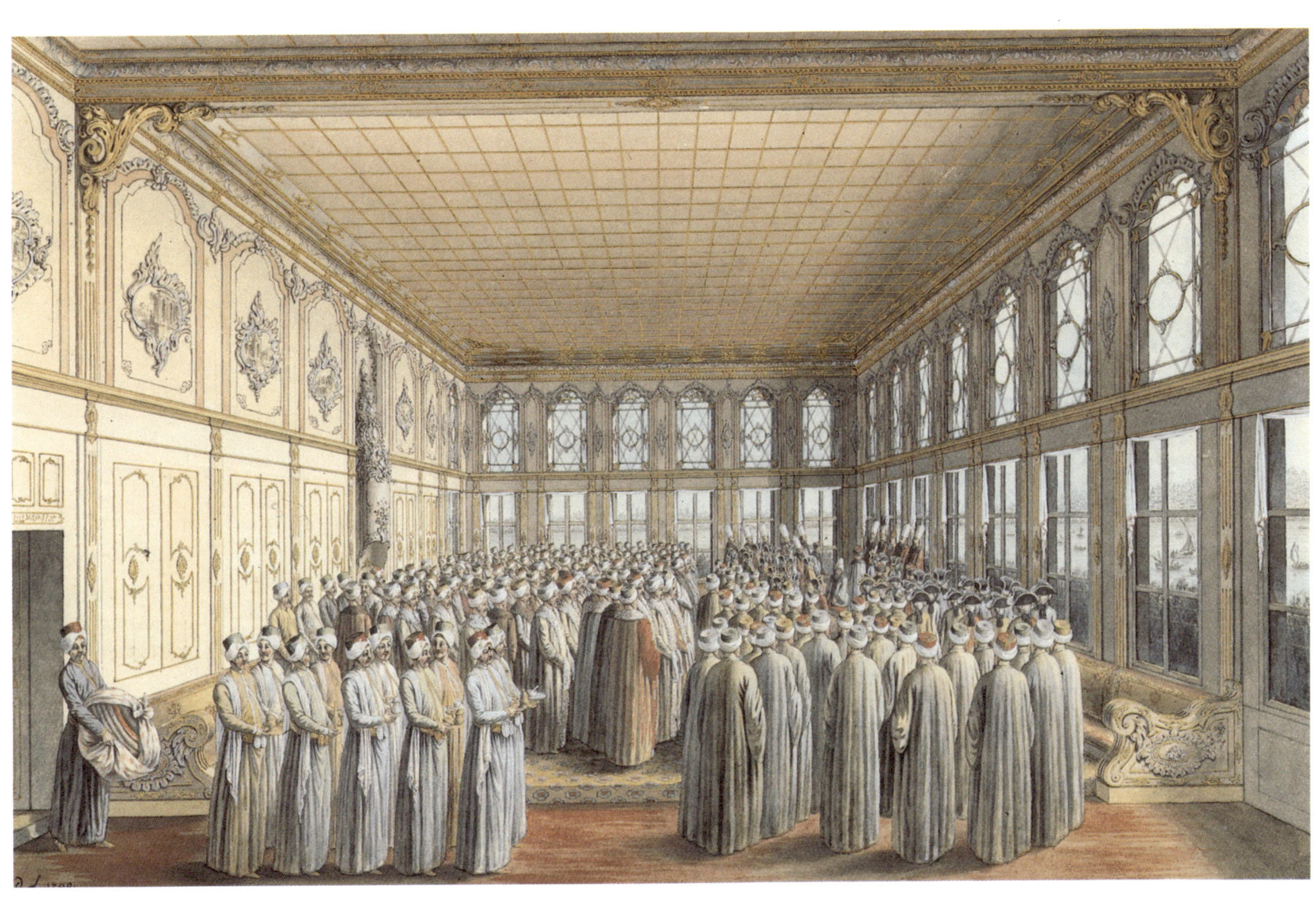

# 8. *Chamber of a Minister of the Ottoman Empire,* 1788

Pen and black ink, brown and gray wash, over black chalk. 10⅛ × 15 inches (257 × 380 mm).

Signed and dated in pen and brown ink, at lower right, *J. M. Moreau Lejne 1788.*

WATERMARK: D & C Blauw.

PROVENANCE: Sale, Christie's, London, 13–14 December 1984, lot 128; acquired from Didier Aaron, Inc., New York.

2001.2

Moreau primarily devoted his career to making prints, first after works by other artists, then eventually after his own drawings, as well as designs for book illustrations. He achieved official success by 1770, when he was named *dessinateur des menus plaisirs du roi* (designer of the king's entertainments) to Louis XV. In this capacity, and later as *dessinateur et graveur de cabinet du roi* (draftsman and engraver to the king) to Louis XVI, Moreau captured in drawings and prints the splendid events of the court in the waning years of the ancien régime. He was nominated to the Académie royale in 1789, although the Revolution eliminated official patronage. He emerged after the Revolution as a drawing instructor at the École centrale with a flourishing career as a book illustrator, before being reinstated by Louis XVIII shortly before his death to apply his skills chronicling the events of the nascent regime.

As was noted by Cara Dufour Denison, this drawing was among those by Moreau preparatory for illustrations to Ignace Mouradja d'Ohsson's (1740–1807) *Tableau général de l'Empire Othoman* and was engraved by Georges Malbeste (*Appartement d'un Ministre de la Porte, Partie Morale;* vol. 2, 1790, pl. 62). D'Ohsson was an Armenian Ottoman in Swedish diplomatic service in Constantinople who wrote about the Mongol empire; his *Tableau général* remains a major monument among Ottoman and Turkish studies. The three published volumes contain 237 engraved illustrations, which document the events and people described in the text. D'Ohsson had been amassing material for the book since 1764. Twenty years later, he left Constantinople for Paris, where he finished and published it.

The present drawing is dated 1788, when Moreau's talents had reached full maturity and his experience depicting interior scenes with large numbers of figures had been well developed. For such a precise drawing, there is very little underdrawing, although the pinpricks and ruled lines reveal Moreau's mastery of drafting tools. It is not believed that Moreau traveled to the Levant; Auguste Boppe suggested that many of the drawings in the *Tableau général* were based on designs by indigenous artists (see Boppe 1911, p. 153). D'Ohsson's correspondence indicates that an Ottoman Greek, Kapidagli Konstantin, and his shop, were the source of many original compositions. In the end, however, it was Moreau's delicately detailed drawing, down to the plumes of pipe smoke and patterned robes, that provided d'Ohsson's text with its visual counterpart.

JT

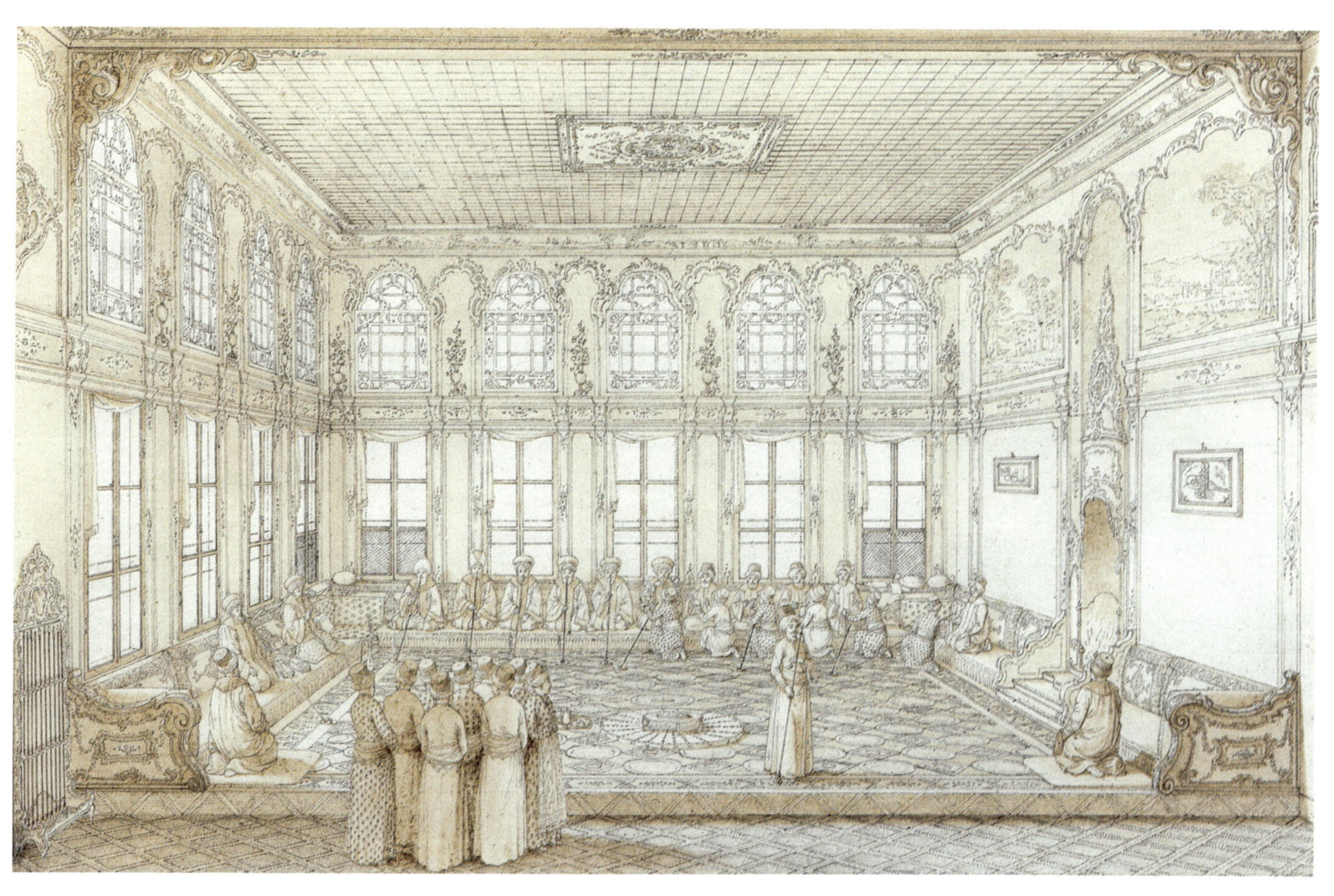

FRANÇOIS ANDRÉ VINCENT French, Paris 1746–1816 Paris

# 9. *A Group of Elegantly Dressed Gentlemen*, ca. 1778

Pen and brown ink and brown wash, over black chalk. 16⅛ × 19 inches (410 × 480 mm).

PROVENANCE: Sale, Étude Bisman, Rouen, 6 November 1994, lot 50; acquired from Thomas Williams Fine Art, London, and W. M. Brady & Co., New York.

EXHIBITION: New York 1995, no. 41.

1998.14

Vincent was one of the leading French artists of the late eighteenth century, recognized for his talent in portraying both classical and historical scenes. He won the Prix de Rome in 1768, and spent the years 1771–75 at the French Academy in Rome under Charles-Joseph Natoire. He also traveled with fellow artist Jean-Honoré Fragonard (1732–1806) and developed a bravura style of wash drawing. After returning to France, he was provisionally accepted by the Académie royale in 1777 and exhibited fifteen paintings at the Salon that year. Vincent continued to show regularly at the Salon and was formally received into the Académie in 1782. His success continued throughout the Revolution, and his studio became one of the most popular in Paris.

This drawing is one of three known studies for the painting *The Marquis de la Galaizière Created Chancellor of Lorraine at the Château of Meudon by King Stanislaus of Poland, 18 January 1737* (Fig. 1). This work, along with its pendant, *The New Chancellor Receiving Homage from the First President of the Sovereign Court of Lorraine at Nancy, March 21, 1737*, was commissioned in 1778 by the marquis, Antoine-Martin Chaumont de La Galaizière (1697–1783), to decorate his château, Marleil-le-Guyon, and to celebrate his former role as chancellor. From 1733, when the duchy of Lorraine was ceded to the Polish king Stanislaus for his lifetime, until 1766, when the area was annexed by France, the marquis served as Louis XV's appointed chancellor to the Polish king.

The present drawing is preparatory for the group of observers in front of and to the left of the column in the middle ground of the painting. The figures to the right of the column are the subject of another sheet in a French private collection (Cuzin 1987, fig. 33). The group of gentlemen surrounding King Stanislaus, in the left foreground, is depicted in a drawing in Montpellier (Musée Atger, A 5V 27; Nancy 2004, p. 118).

The drawing depicts nine figures: in the painting Vincent omitted the man second from left who is barely visible in the drawing. The sheet also contains at right a very summary black chalk outline of the female figure that appears to the right of the abbé in the painting. The three most prominent figures in the Morgan drawing have been identified by Pierre Boyé as family members of the marquis (from right to left): Henri-Ignace, abbé de La Galaizière; Jean-Baptiste, comte de Luçay; and *president* de Marguerit (Boyé 1936, pp. 542–43). Vincent's talents as a portraitist as well as his bold brush style are very much evident in this sheet, which reveals his exceptional talent at the outset of his career.

JT

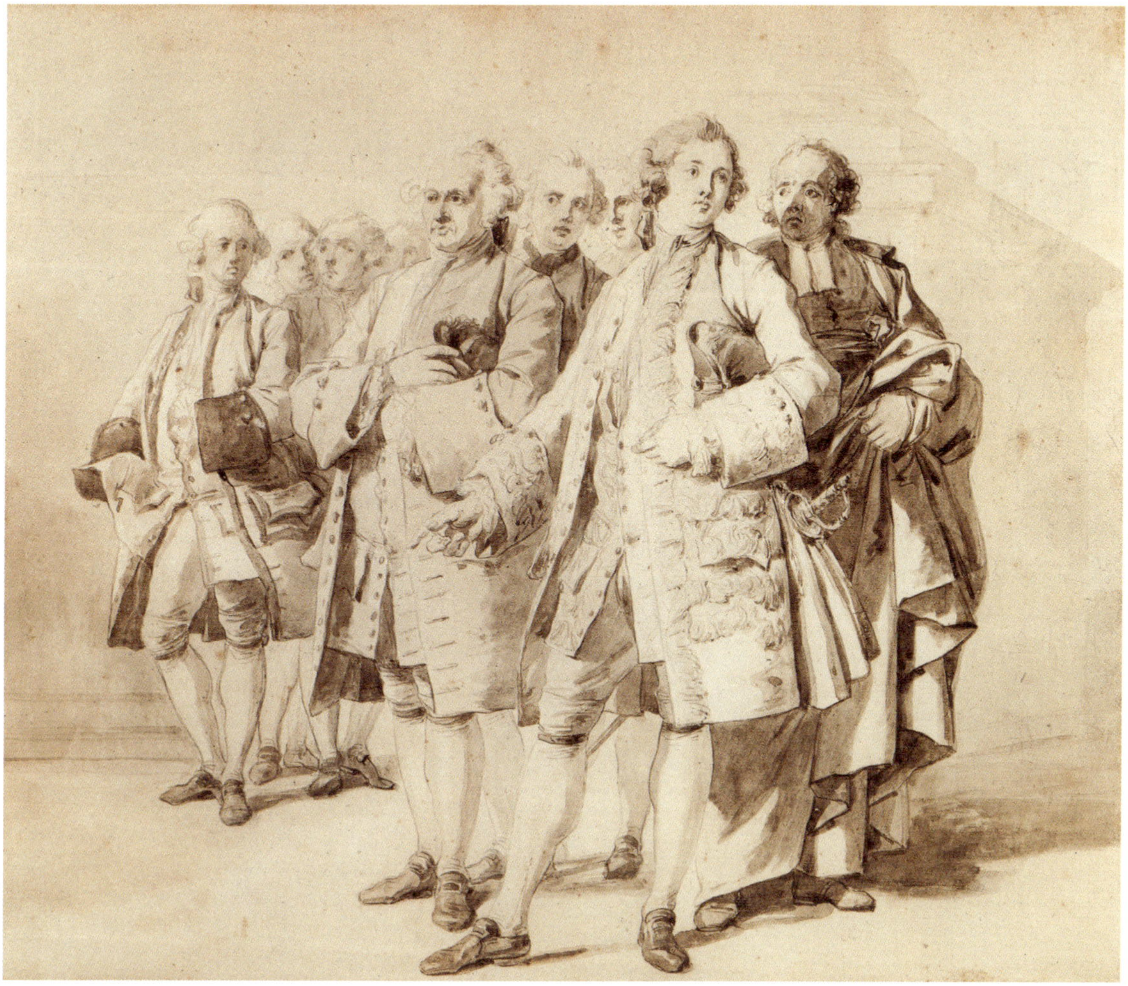

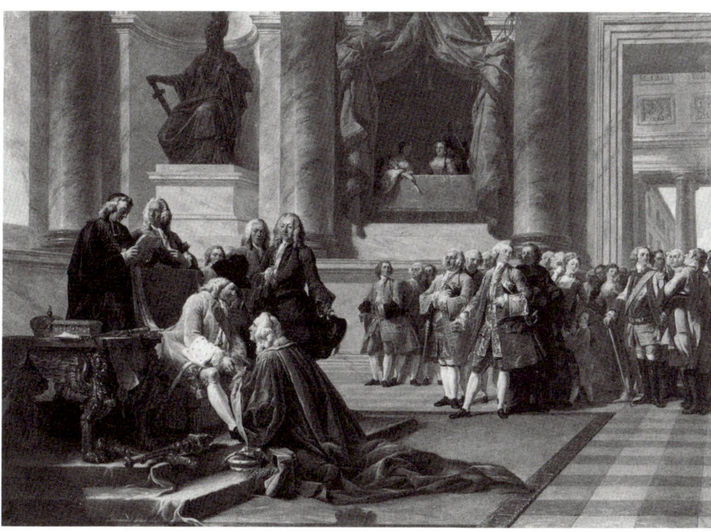

Fig. 1. François André Vincent, *The Marquis de la Galaizière Created Chancellor of Lorraine at the Château of Meudon by King Stanislaus of Poland, 18 January 1737* (Musée du château de Versailles, on deposit at the Musée Historique Lorrain, Nancy)

# 10. *A Capriccio of Classical Ruins with Figures, Including a Sybil*

Pen and brown ink, point of brush and gray wash, brown wash, over black chalk; laid down on Mariette mount. 9⅛ × 14³⁄₁₆ inches (234 × 360 mm).

Signed at lower left, in pen and brown ink, *J. Po Panini*, inscribed by the artist at lower center, *P.r Mr Mariette*, and inscribed on mount in cartouche, *Joan. Pauli / Panini*; inscribed on verso of old mount at upper center in graphite, *Joan. Pauli Panini.*

PROVENANCE: Pierre-Jean Mariette (1694–1774; Lugt 1852); his sale, 15 November 1775–31 January 1776, lot 564; private collection, Sweden; acquired from Artemis Fine Arts Limited, London.

EXHIBITION: New York 2004, no. 20.

2004.21

The foremost Roman painter of real and imaginary architectural views of his day, Panini served as professor of perspective at the French Academy for thirty years until his death in 1765. He is best known for his *vedute*, or view paintings, of Rome and *capricci*, or imagined designs, of Roman classical monuments, both immensely popular with French and British collectors on the Grand Tour.

The present drawing represents a *capriccio* of a group of figures amid classical ruins and buildings reminiscent of actual Roman sites. These include at left the Temple of the Sybil, Tivoli, and at right the pyramidal Tomb of Caius Cestius, Rome. The outsized marble urn at upper right is an amalgam of the celebrated Medici and Borghese vases.

Panini was adept at rearranging the same motifs in very different ways in compositions of great charm. He utilized the general composition and several motifs in this drawing in three paintings, of which the closest to the present sheet is *The Sybil* of about 1750 in the Musée de Beaux-Arts, Valence, on deposit from the Musée du Louvre, Paris (Fig. 1). The others, both entitled *Preaching of a Sybil*, are of almost identical composition. One is in the Cassa di Risparmio di Parma e Piacenza in Piacenza and is dated about 1739 (Paris and elsewhere 1993, no. 37); the other, dated about 1740, is in the Louvre, Paris (Paris and elsewhere 1993, no. 10).

The Morgan drawing is one of thirty-five sheets attributed to Panini and described in the catalogue of the 1775 sale of the collection of Pierre-Jean Mariette (nos. 548–74), the great eighteenth-century *amateur* and collector. Laid down on its original Mariette mount, the drawing bears an inscription in Panini's hand dedicating it to the French collector. It is the third drawing by Panini from the Mariette collection to be acquired for the Morgan on the Sunny Crawford von Bülow Fund (1982.18:1–2; New York 1996, nos. 34a–b). KS

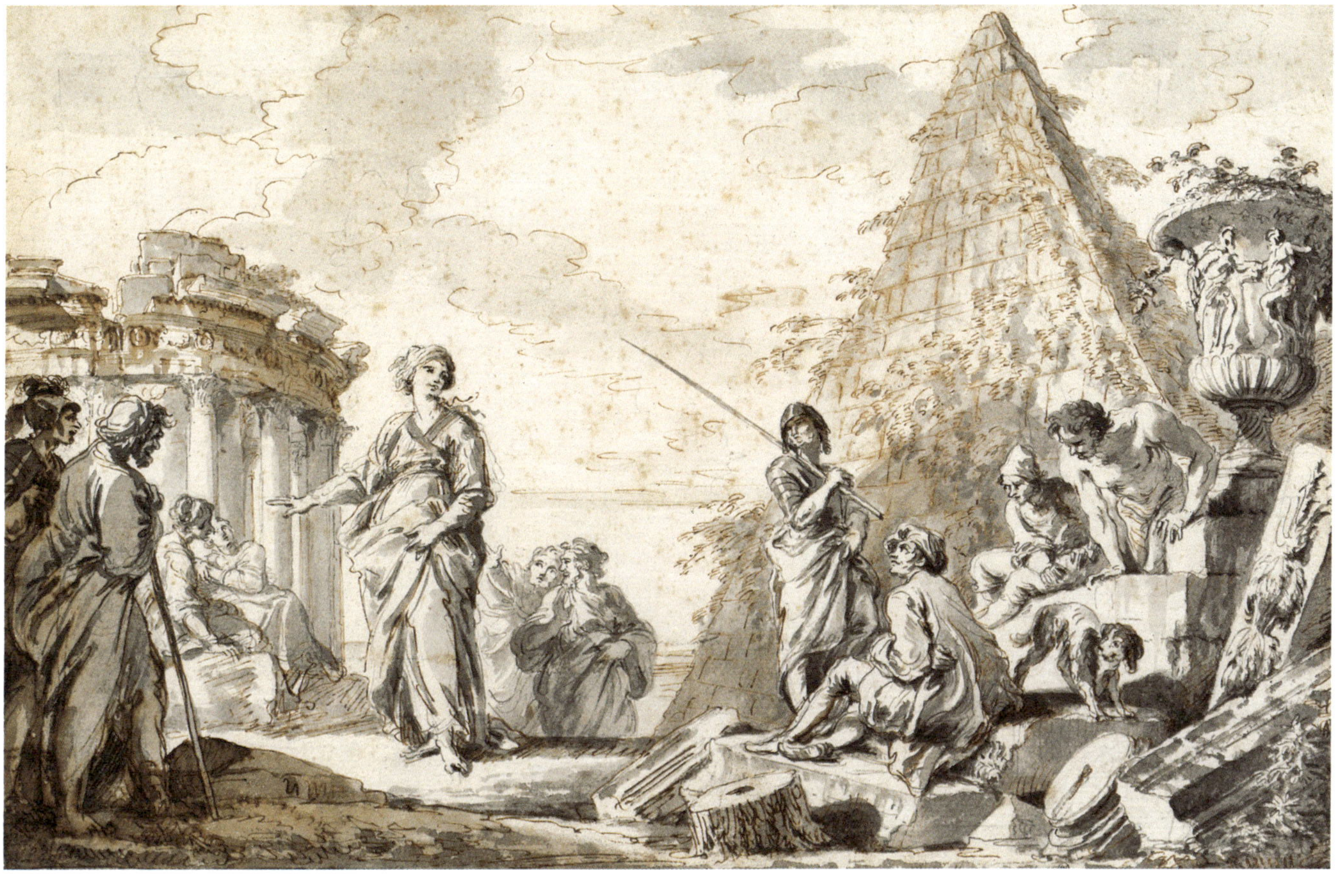

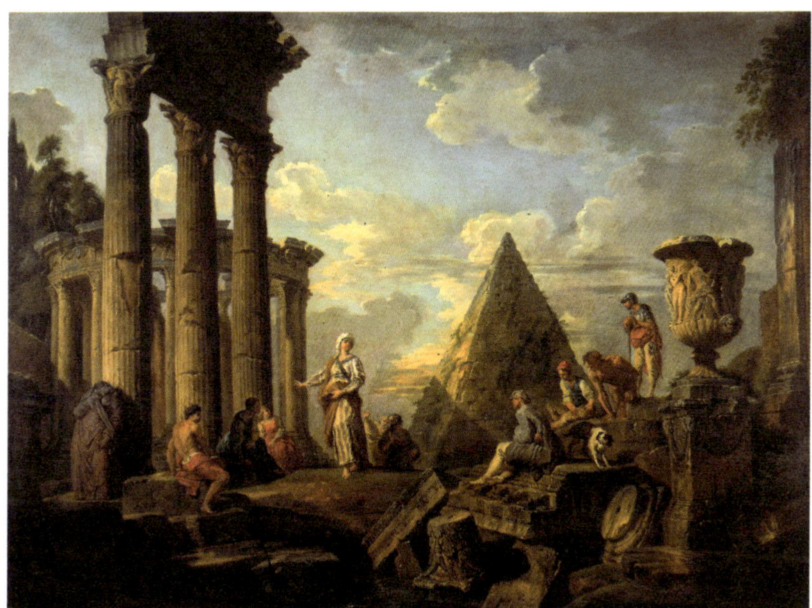

Fig. 1. Giovanni Paolo Panini, *Sibilla* (Musée du Louvre, Paris, on deposit at the Musée de Beaux-Arts, Valence)

FRANCESCO PANINI Italian, Rome ca. 1725–after 1794 Rome

# 11. *Interior of St. Peter's: The Portico*

Watercolor with shell gold over gesso, over outline etching. Design area: 19⅝ × 31½ inches (498 × 800 mm); sheet: 22⅞ × 34 9/16 inches (582 × 877 mm).

Inscribed below design at lower left in pen and black ink, *Francesco Panini fece, e Vende in Roma,* and inscribed at lower center, / / *Prospetto Interno del' Portico della Basilica di S. Pietro nel Vaticano* / / .

PROVENANCE: Presumably bought from the artist; by descent in the Öttingen-Wallerstein family, Maihingen, Bavaria, Germany (see Lugt suppl. 2715a), until 1997 (the foregoing according to New York 1997); acquired from Artemis Fine Arts Inc., New York.

EXHIBITION: New York 1997, no. 29.

1997.7

Francesco Panini was the son and pupil of the famed view painter Giovanni Paolo Panini (see No. 10). Very little information about Francesco's career has survived, but it is known that he served as his father's principal studio assistant (Philadelphia and Houston 2000, p. 417), making preparatory drawings for engravings after the elder Panini's paintings. He also collaborated with printmakers, including the engraver Giovanni Volpato (see No. 12), for whom he provided drawings to be translated into outline etchings that he then hand colored in watercolor (London and Rome 1996–97, p. 46). Through the prints made after Francesco's drawings, the elder Panini's paintings became known throughout Europe. One such work, a drawing by Francesco Panini after a painting by his father—*A Panoramic View of Rome from Monte Mario* (Stiftung Preussische Schlösser und Gärten, Potsdam; London and Rome 1996–97, no. 6)—engraved by Volpato in 1779, was used frequently in souvenir and guidebooks to the papal city until the end of the eighteenth century (London and Rome 1996–97, p. 46).

The present sheet is derived from an oil painting of about 1750 by the elder Panini, *Portico of St. Peter's* (Casita del Principe, Escorial; Arisi 1986, no. 399). While carefully following the general design of the painting, the younger Panini broadened and deepened the composition to be more fully panoramic, both horizontally and vertically, encompassing more than the eye could see in a single glance and emphasizing the monumental scale of the space and its awe-inspiring effect. Generously brushed shell gold, applied over gesso to suggest three-dimensionality, creates a sumptuous effect and gives some idea of the value such works represented to collectors.

KS

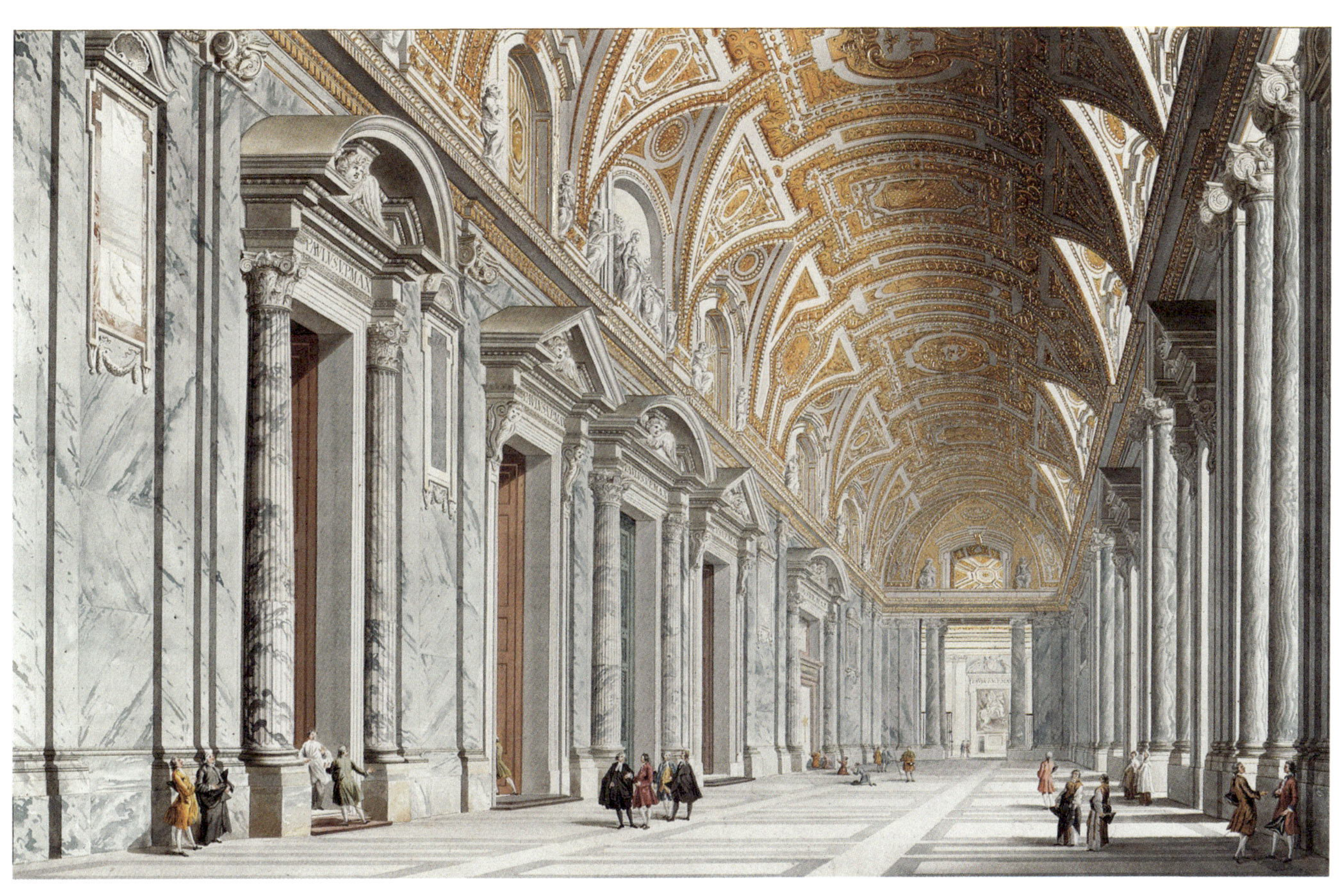

LOUIS DUCROS Swiss, Moudon 1748–1810 Lausanne

GIOVANNI VOLPATO Italian, Angarano di Bassano 1740–1803 Rome

# 12. *View of the Temple of the Sybil, Tivoli*

Watercolor over outline etching; laid down on old mount. 20 1/8 × 28 11/16 inches (510 × 729 mm).

Inscribed at lower right in pen and brown ink, *Le temple de la Sibille Tivoli*, on old mount at lower left, *Volpato, et Ducros*, and at center, *Vue du Temple de la Sibille à Tivoli*.

PROVENANCE: Presumably bought from the artist; by descent in the Öttingen-Wallerstein family, Maihingen, Bavaria, Germany (see Lugt suppl. 2715a), until 1997 (the foregoing according to New York 1997); acquired from Artemis Fine Arts Inc., New York.

EXHIBITION: New York 1997, no. 28.

1997.8

Born in Switzerland, Ducros trained in Geneva before traveling to Rome in 1776. There he quickly established himself as a specialist in large, highly finished topographical landscapes in watercolor, which were prized for their realism by visitors on the Grand Tour. In 1779 Ducros entered into a partnership with the printmaker Giovanni Volpato to produce engraved souvenir views of Rome. Volpato, who had settled in Rome in 1771, was famous for his engravings after Raphael's frescoes in the Vatican *logge*. The partnership of Ducros and Volpato flourished, and in 1780 they issued their first series of prints, *Vues de Rome et des ses environs*, which was published in Rome to great commercial success.

The present sheet was a collaboration of the two artists, employing the method devised by Ducros to create multiple impressions of the same subject. He would execute the original design and produce an outline etching from which several impressions would be printed. For each design he also made a watercolor drawing to be used as a model for hand coloring the etchings, which was carried out either by Volpato's assistants or by Ducros himself. Another impression of the present design is in the collection of the Musée cantonal des Beaux-Arts, Lausanne (Kenwood and elsewhere 1985–86, no. 20). The whereabouts of the watercolor model is not known.

The work seen here depicts a view of the ancient city of Tivoli, on the Aniene River about twenty miles east of Rome. Famed for its picturesque terrain and dramatic waterfall, Tivoli was one of the most popular destinations for travelers on the Grand Tour. It was also the site of the first-century B.C. Temple of the Sybil, seen here in the center of the composition. The temple was a frequent subject for artists of the day, who commonly focused on it as an architectural ruin—for example, the engraving by Giovanni Battista Piranesi (1720–1778) in which the temple is isolated and seen in foreshortened view from below (Wilton-Ely 1994, no. 196)—or as an emblem of classical antiquity set in an ideal landscape—as in Richard Wilson's painting of about 1754, *Landscape Capriccio on the Via Aemilia, with the Temple of the Sybil at Tivoli and the Broken Bridge at Narni* (collection of Mr. and Mrs. Brian Thomas; London 1982–83, no. 73, pl. 3). By contrast, Ducros represented the temple as unidealized, viewed from the side instead of head-on, and blending into the neighboring buildings and verdant surroundings, with a group of figures in the foreground engaged in the activities of daily life. Ducros depicted the temple in at least two other finished watercolors, both viewed from the river upstream from the falls (Musée cantonal des Beaux-Arts, Lausanne; Kenwood and elsewhere 1985–86, nos. 18, 19). KS

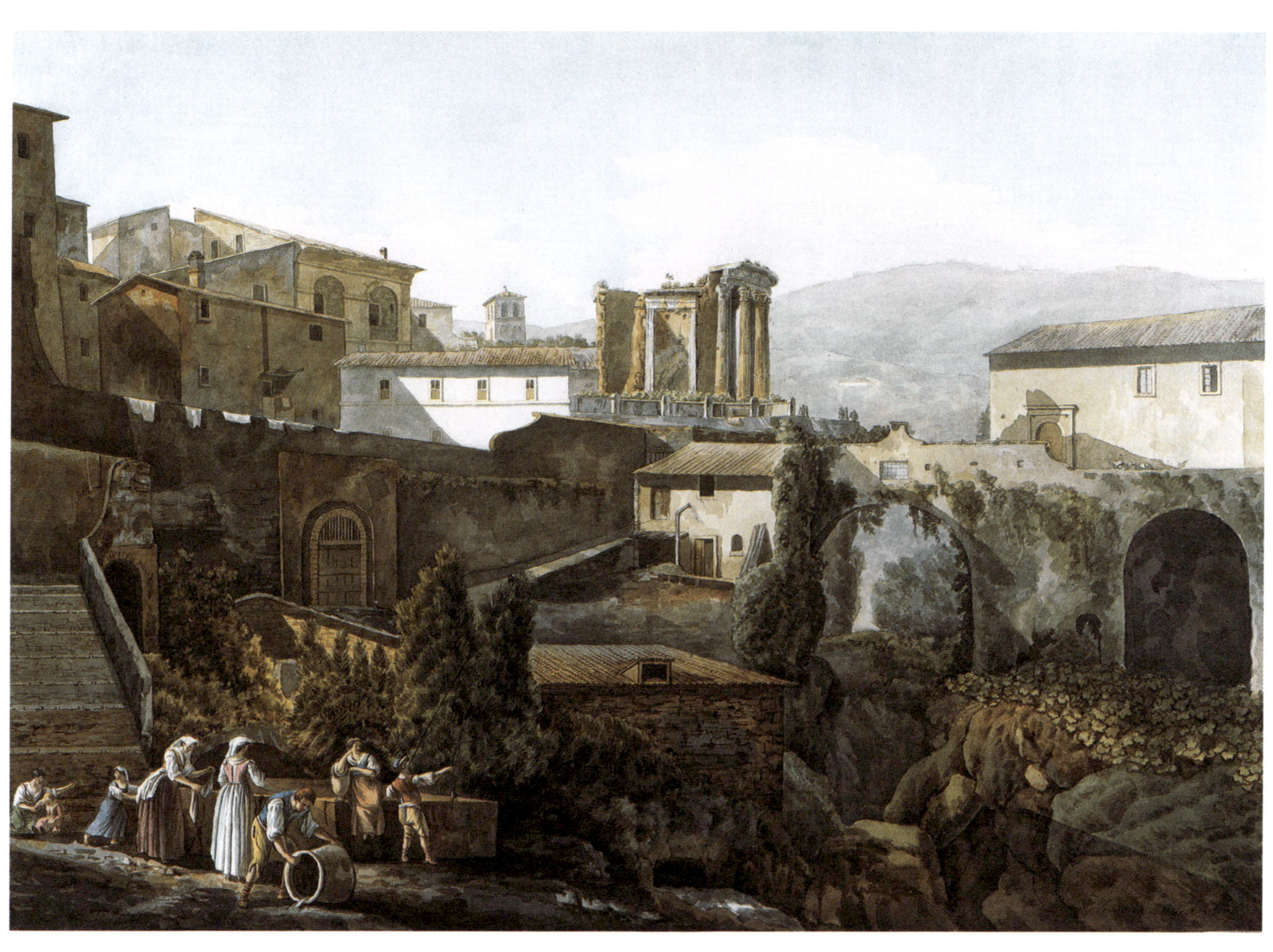

JEAN-BAPTISTE-CLAUDE CHATELAIN British, London 1710–1758 London

# 13. *A Classical Landscape*

Black and white chalks on light brown paper; laid down on old mount. 10⁵⁄₁₆ × 13⅜ inches (262 × 339 mm).

PROVENANCE: Wyndham Payne, The Hermitage, Sidmouth, Devon (1958); sale, Bonham's, Bath (U.K.), 30 January 2006, lot 105, not repr.; acquired from W/S Fine Art Ltd., London.

2006.7

An engraver, draftsman, and drawing master of French Huguenot descent, Chatelain was one of the most accomplished and successful landscape engravers working in mid-eighteenth-century London. Almost nothing of his early life and training is known, but he is said to have served in the French army and probably settled in England during the 1730s (Alexander [forthcoming]). His earliest known works date from that decade, including the drawing manual *A New Book of Landskips* (London, 1737) and *View of Richmond Palace*, a drawing in the Royal Collection at Windsor Castle (London 1984, no. C6), whose figures and their placement in the landscape display a familiarity with the prints of Antoine Watteau (1684–1721). By the 1740s Chatelain was much in demand and produced drawings and provided etchings for numerous projects, including *Forty-Four Italian Landscapes* (1741–43) and *Six Views in the North of England* (1754). He also traveled around Britain making drawings of private houses and estates to be engraved for printed series, among them *Sixteen Perspective Views of Stow* (London, 1753). A copy of this work is preserved in the Morgan collection (PML 53029), and its preparatory drawings are in the Yale Center for British Art, New Haven.

The present drawing represents a mountainous coastal landscape that unfolds beyond a forested headland and a foreground *repoussoir* of dense vegetation. Its location has not been identified and likely is an imagined view. Whereas Chatelain's drawings for prints are often rapidly sketched on small sheets in pen and black ink (see, for example, Kupferstichkabinett, Berlin, nos. 14961–70), the size and high degree of finish of the drawing seen here suggest that it was executed as an independent work for the market or as a gift to a collector. A drawing of a similar subject in the same media and of similar dimensions as the Morgan sheet, recently on the art market, may have been created as a pendant to it or as part of a series of independent works (London 2001a, no. 1).

Various motifs used in the present drawing recall Watteau's copies after the landscapes of Domenico Campagnola (1500–1564), many of which were engraved by François Boucher (1703–1770). For example, the steeply rising mountains, hilltop buildings, and arcaded bridge in the present drawing find counterparts in such sheets by Watteau as *River Landscape with a Fortified Town and Distant Mountains* in the Morgan's collection (1995.1; Rosenberg and Prat 1996, no. 344) and *A Group of Figures with Chariots in a Landscape* in the Rijksmuseum, Amsterdam (Rosenberg and Prat 1996, no. 252). Further, the large tree at right and the densely planted foreground seen here are also to be found in a work such as *Landscape with a Church Behind an Escarpment*, engraved by Boucher after a lost Watteau drawing (Watteau, no. 230; Rosenberg and Prat 1996, no. G 90).

KS

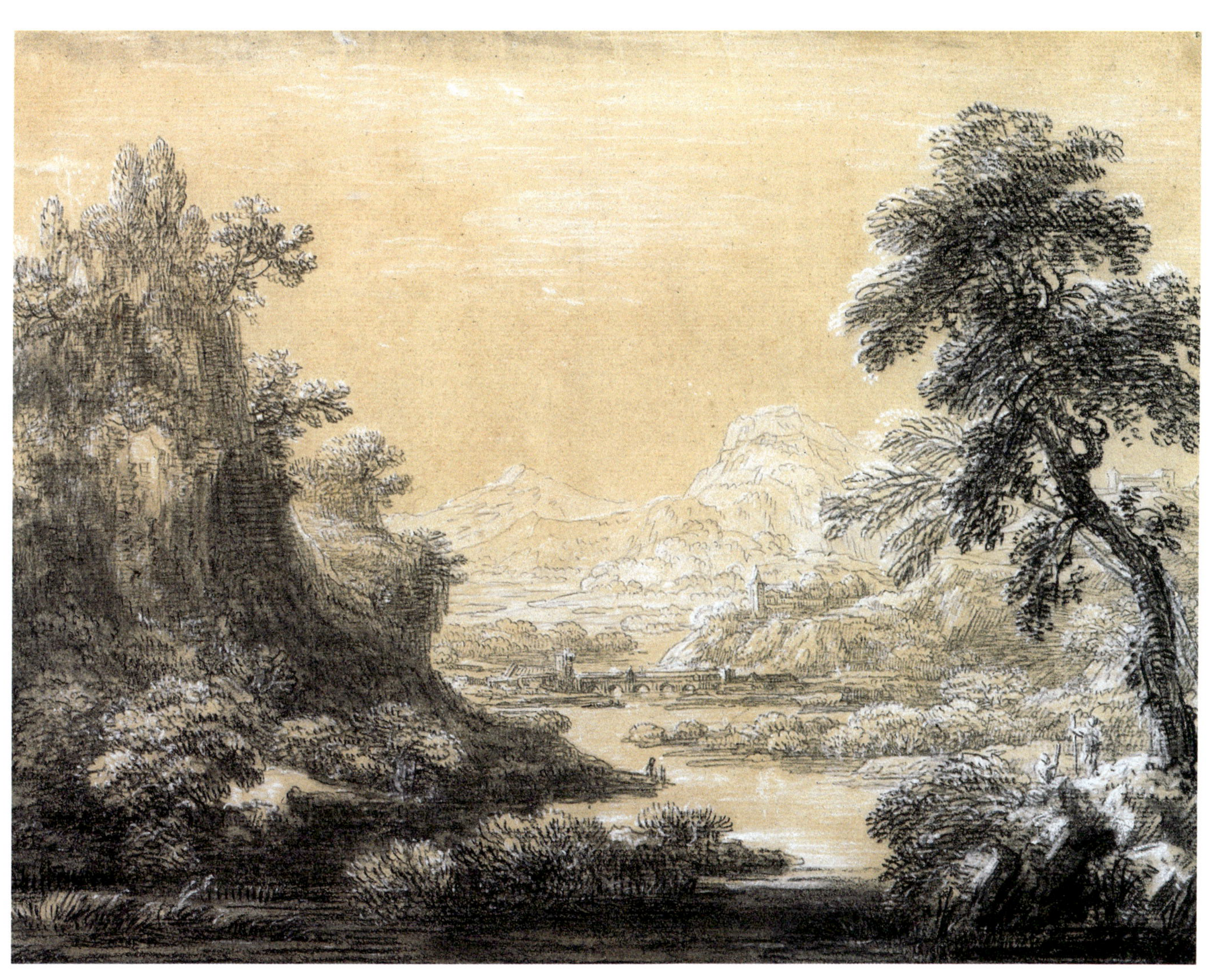

# 14. *The Temple of Bacchus*, 1754

Black chalk and stump, heightened with white chalk, on pale gray paper; laid down on the artist's original mount. 10¾ × 16½ inches (273 × 419 mm).

Signed and dated by the artist on old mount at lower left, *RW. f Romae 1754*, and numbered at lower right, *N°. 9.*; inscribed on small paper label affixed to old mount, *Temple / of / Bacchus*; on verso of original backing paper at upper right in pen and black ink, *49*, at upper left in graphite, *7395 GWGA*.

PROVENANCE: William Legge, 2nd Earl of Dartmouth (1731–1801); by descent to William, 7th Earl of Dartmouth; his sale, Christie's, London, 29 January 1954, lot 11; from which acquired by Thomas Agnew & Sons Ltd., London; from which acquired by C. L. Loyd, Lockinge, Oxfordshire; acquired from Thomas Agnew & Sons Ltd., London.

BIBLIOGRAPHY: Ford 1948, p. 345; Ford 1951, pp. 29, 59, no. 52, pl. 52; Constable 1953, p. 99 (not repr.); Russell 1991, no. 138, p. 49, pl. 56.

EXHIBITIONS: Birmingham 1948–49, no. 78 (not repr.); London 1949, no. 77.

2004.43

The founder of the British landscape school, Richard Wilson began his career as a portraitist but was encouraged by Francesco Zuccarelli (1702–1788) to paint landscapes while on a sojourn in Venice in 1750. He soon had several important commissions from British nobility who admired his talent for combining plein-air naturalism with the Arcadian ideal landscape perfected by Claude Lorrain (1600–1682). One of those commissions was from the 2nd Earl of Dartmouth, who in 1752 or 1753 engaged Wilson to produce a suite of sixty-eight finished landscape drawings in the artist's signature medium of black chalk on gray or blue paper. The present drawing is number forty-nine of the group, and that number appears on the verso of the original backing paper.

Executed in Rome in 1754, the sheet is on the original mount with its lilac-wash border, which was colored by the artist himself or under his direction. The buildings represented are, at center, the ruins of the Constantinian basilica of Sant' Agnese; behind it to the right, the fourth-century church of Santa Costanza; and, to the left, the seventh-century church of Sant' Agnese fuori le Mura. Wilson's inscription *Temple of Bacchus* on the mount, which provided the traditional title for the drawing, reflected the then-current name of Santa Costanza.

The antique sarcophagus in the foreground may have been connected to a sketch by Wilson; he routinely chose subjects from his sketchbooks for inclusion in his finished landscapes. He probably added the sarcophagus as an allusion to classical antiquity, which would have been understood and appreciated by his sophisticated patron.

The overall design reveals both the influence of Claude Lorrain, whose works Wilson studied closely during his years in Rome, and Wilson's legacy to the next two generations of British landscape artists, most especially John Robert Cozens (see Nos. 18–19) and J. M. W. Turner (see Nos. 24–25). Some of that legacy can be found in the large tree at right used as a framing device, the foreground *repoussoir* with figures set before the view, and the view itself bathed in light. Wilson executed a less elaborate drawing of the same subject from a slightly different angle, in which the basilica ruins are the most prominent element in the composition (Ashmolean Museum, Oxford; Solkin 1978, pl. 18a).

A close correspondence exists between the outline of Santa Costanza in the present drawing and that in a print by Piranesi, *Sezione I. Avanzo della gran Fabbrica sepolcrale, aggiunta al Mausoleo di Costanza . . .*, from *Le Antichità Romane*, published in 1756 (Wilton-Ely 1994, no. 379, p. 431). Both diverge considerably from the actual profile of the building, most particularly the round tower, which in the Morgan drawing and the etching is taller and more slender than in the Ashmolean drawing or in reality.

KS

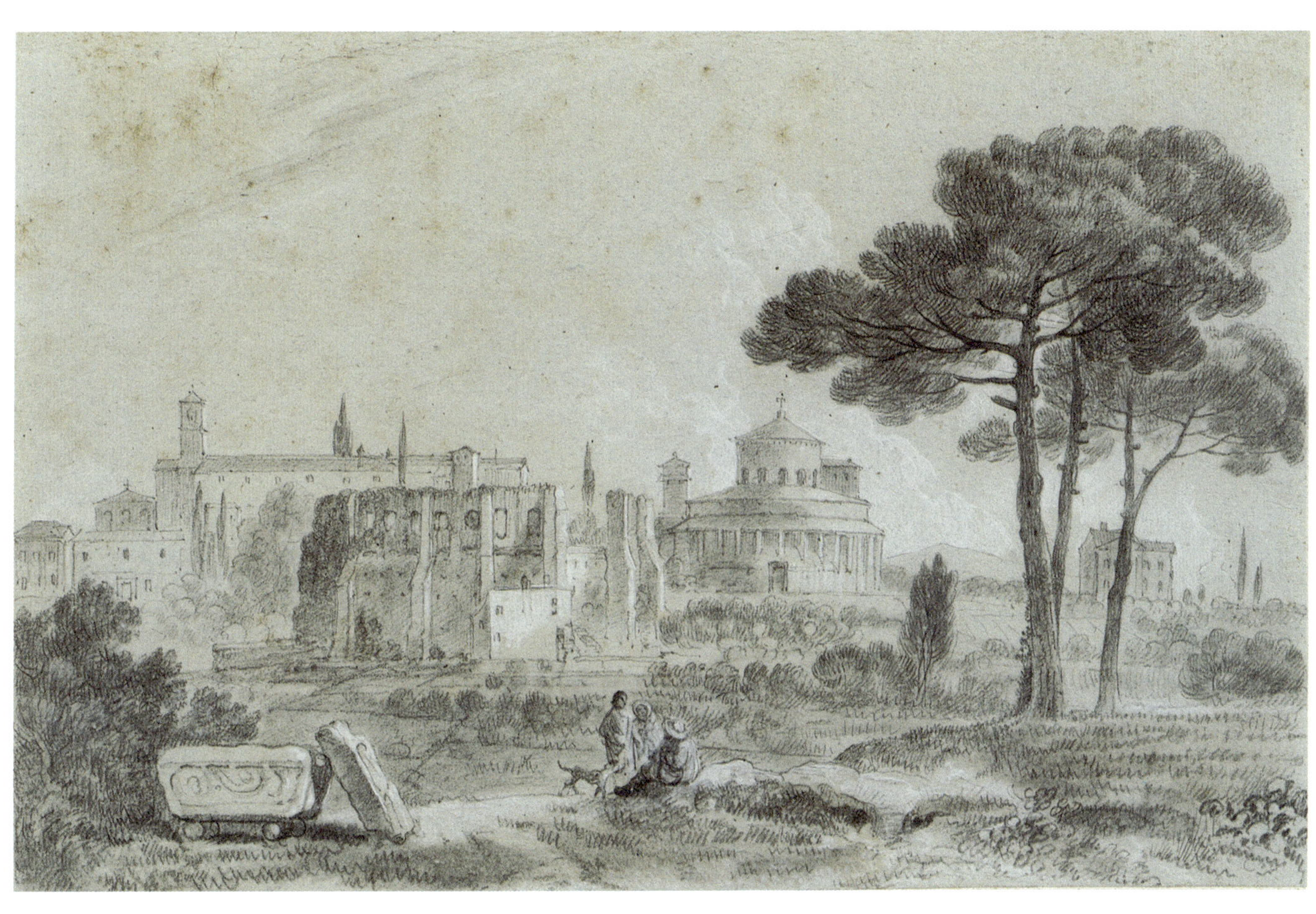

# 15. *The Old English Bridge at Shrewsbury Under Reconstruction*

Watercolor over graphite; laid down.
13¼ × 26 inches (337 × 660 mm).

Inscribed in pen and black ink at lower right, *the old Bridge at Shrewsbury etc [?]*.

PROVENANCE: Sale, Christie's, London, 15 June 1982, lot 121 (incorrectly described as the "Welsh" bridge); private collection; acquired from Thomas Agnew & Sons Ltd., London.

EXHIBITION: London 2002, no. 9.

2002.67

Paul Sandby trained with his older brother, Thomas (1721–1798). From 1747 to 1752 he served as a military draftsman making topographical drawings and maps in Scotland. Back in London in 1752 he began teaching drawing and produced landscapes in watercolor and oil inspired by seventeenth-century Dutch art. In 1760 he helped found the Society of Artists and eight years later was the only watercolorist elected a founding member of the Royal Academy of Art. Often referred to as "the father of English watercolour" (Wilton 1977, p. 11), Sandby played a key role in raising the status of the watercolor medium to a level comparable to that of oil painting.

Sandby's first visit to Shrewsbury, on the Severn River in Shropshire in western England, likely was in 1770, the year of his earliest dated views of the town. One of these is reproduced in his aquatint of 1779, *Part of the Old Bridge at Shrewsbury with Two Arches of the New One, 1770*. The present drawing may have been the model for the print, which records the same view with minor variations. The bridges of Shrewsbury were among Sandby's favorite subjects, and he made at least thirteen watercolor drawings of the structures (London 2002). The English Bridge, whose origins date to the early Middle Ages, is shown here with its medieval gatehouse at right and mill buildings at center. To their left are two arches of the new bridge under construction. The completed new bridge caught the eye of J. M. W. Turner, who made a drawing of it dated about 1795 (private collection, England; Wilton 1979, no. 136).

With its attention to architectural detail and softly muted palette, the Morgan sheet reflects Sandby's training as a topographer. Its sweeping panorama and dramatic lighting effects signify its ambitions as a finished work of art. During the period in which Sandby made this drawing he was exposed for the first time to the picturesque landscape of northern Wales. Some of the expansiveness of his Welsh views—for example, *The Tide Rising at Britton Ferry* of 1773 (London and Washington 1993, no. 254, pl. 112)—may be observed here.

KS

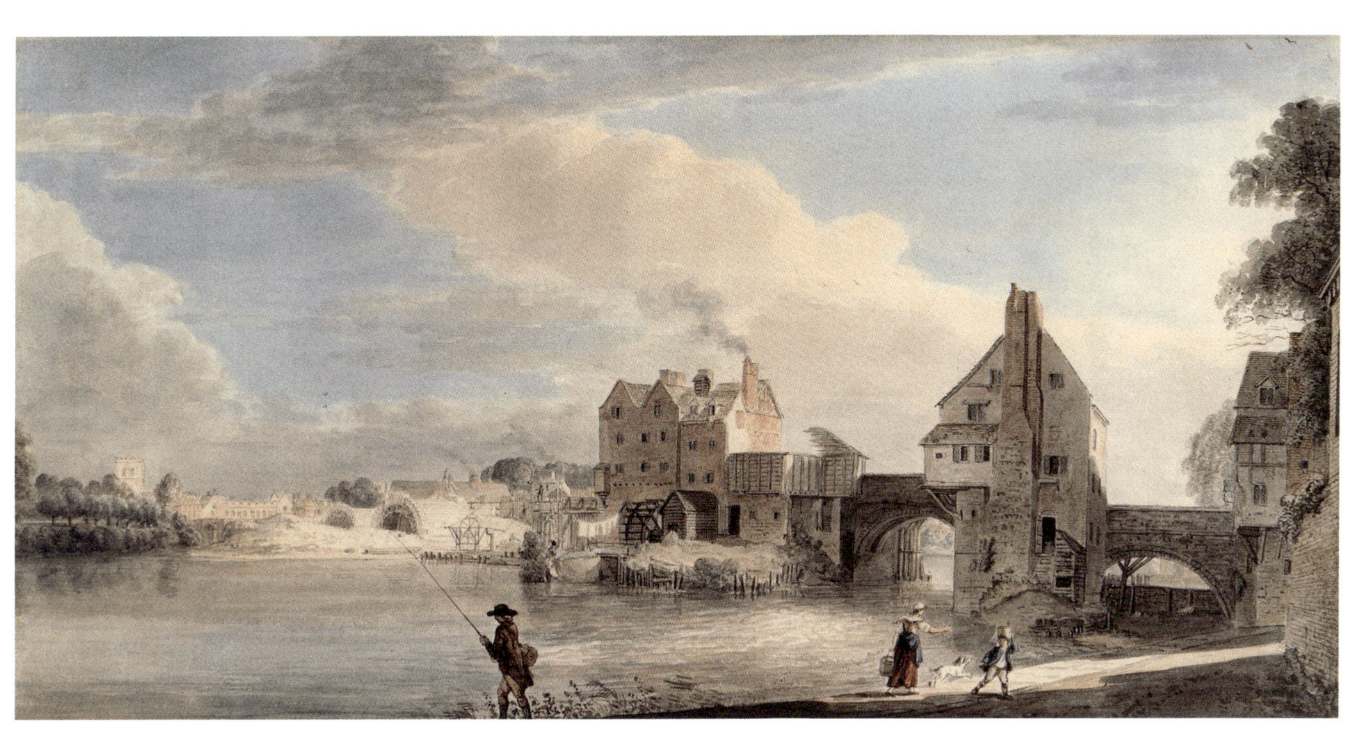

# 16. *View of the Banqueting Hall, Whitehall, and Scotland Yard with Elegant Figures*

Watercolor and white gouache over graphite; lined. 14⁹⁄₁₆ × 21¼ inches (370 × 523 mm).

PROVENANCE: Private collection, Hampshire; acquired from Andrew Clayton-Payne Ltd., London.

Purchased on the Sunny Crawford von Bülow Fund in memory of Sir Paul Getty.

2003.12

Views in and around London were frequent subjects for Paul Sandby, who often represented grand edifices in highly personal ways. *View of the Town Through the Gateway, from the Castle Hill* of about 1770 (Royal Collection, Windsor; New Haven 1985, no. 86) shows not the main entrance of Windsor Castle but a corner of it, with figures riding in a carriage dominating the foreground. The subject of the present drawing is an interior courtyard of the old Whitehall Palace, among the few areas of the complex not destroyed by fire in 1698. The large building in the background at left is the Banqueting House, built by Inigo Jones in 1619–22 and the subject of another Morgan drawing by Jones (1984.29). At center is the medieval Court Gate. The row of low buildings surrounding the courtyard comprised Great Scotland Yard, thought to have been so named because it housed the residences of the visiting Scottish kings and ambassadors before the union of Scotland and England in 1707.

In contrast to Canaletto's grand *View of Whitehall from St. James's Park* of 1749 (formerly Roy Miles Gallery, London; Constable 1976, no. 416, pl. 76), looking east across a lush expanse of park with elegant promenading figures, Sandby's subject presents a view of more humble figures conducting everyday business. Despite the drawing's human atmosphere, its scale and high degree of finish suggest it was made to fulfill a specific commission. Characteristically, Sandby created delicate tonal shifts across the sheet, especially in the brick facades of the buildings at left. The overall effect is rich and varied despite the subdued palette of gray, ocher, and tan.

The date of execution of the drawing is not known, but in 1777 it was engraved by Edward Rooker for John Boydell, one of the leading engravers of the day. Sandby prepared the sheet with at least one study, a watercolor sketch today in the collection of the Guildhall Library, London.

KS

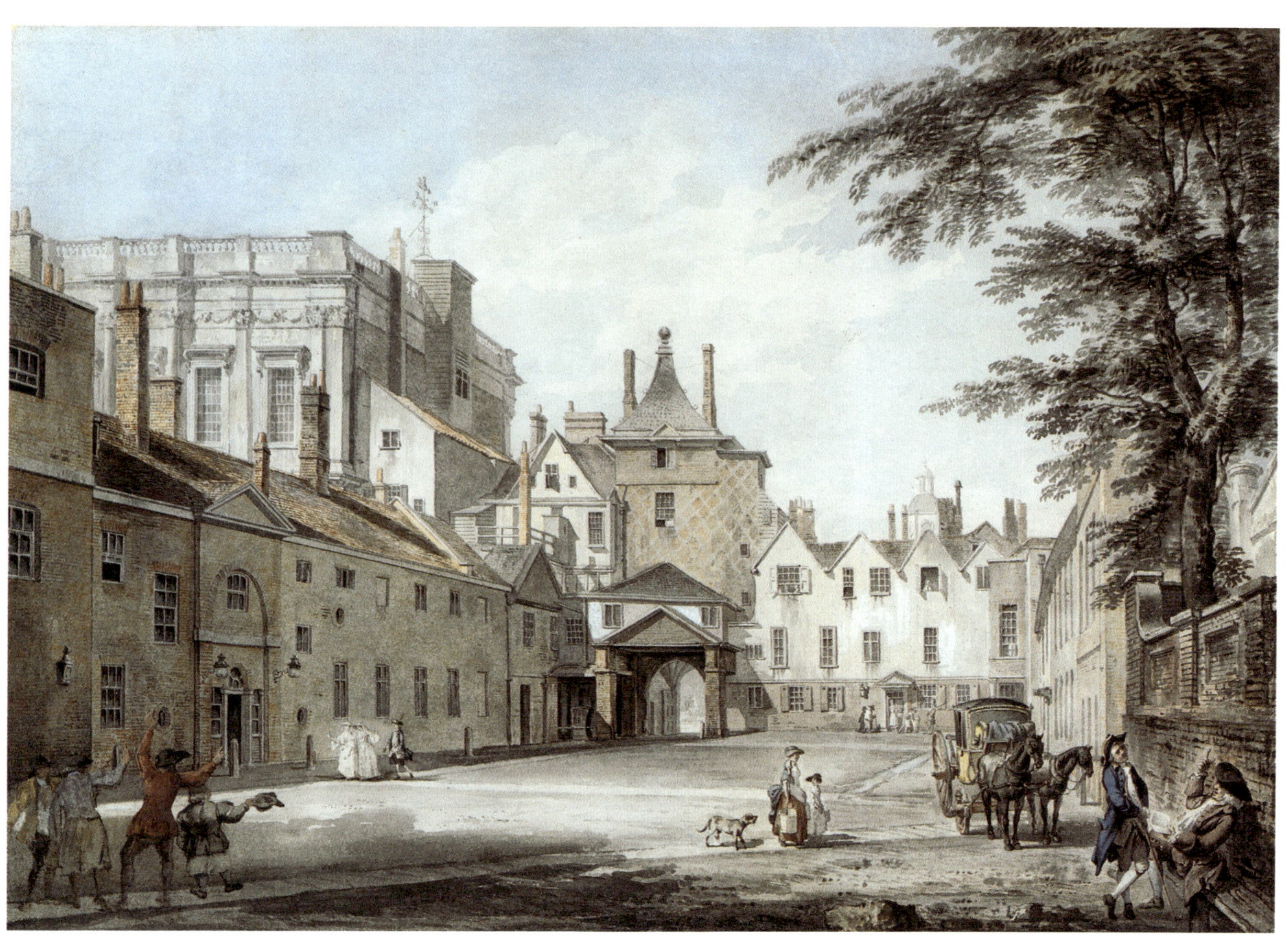

# 17. *Reposo*

Pen and black ink. 11 × 8¼ inches (280 × 210 mm).

PROVENANCE: Leonard Baskin (1922–2000), Northampton, Mass.; from whom purchased by Frederick J. Cummings, New York; by whom consigned to Ronald L. Winokur, Los Angeles; from whom purchased by Mr. and Mrs. Deane F. Johnson, Los Angeles; sale, Christie's, London, 18 November 2004, lot 61; acquired from W. M. Brady & Co., Inc., New York.

BIBLIOGRAPHY: Eastbourne and London 1968, p. 52, under no. 108; Sunderland 1988, p. 187, no. 140.5a, fig. 249.

EXHIBITION: New York 2005, no. 4.

2005.227

A painter, draftsman, and etcher, Mortimer is known for his history painting in the manner of Salvator Rosa (1615–1673), but his work also comprised portraiture, decorative interiors, and book illustration. He entered the London studio of the portrait painter Thomas Hudson (1701–1779) about 1757 and within a few years began to win prizes for his work. In 1765 he was elected to the Society of Artists of Great Britain, becoming its president in 1774. Four years later he was elected to the Royal Academy, an event he marked with the publication on 8 December 1778 of a suite of fifteen etchings after his designs. The present drawing served as the model in reverse for the plate he entitled *Reposo*, or "rest." A drawn copy after the etching, in the same direction, is in the Victoria and Albert Museum, London (Eastbourne and London 1968, no. 108).

Mortimer dedicated the set to Sir Joshua Reynolds (1723–1792), president of the Royal Academy. Among the other subjects in the suite are four allegorical compositions—*Comedy, Tragedy, Pastoral,* and *Elegy*—and several depictions of monsters and *banditti,* the muscular male figures often clothed in armor and bearing weapons that derived from Salvator Rosa and were familiar types in Mortimer's oeuvre. The set also included representations of two artists of opposing temperaments and philosophies: Salvator Rosa, the prototype of the romantic genius, and Gérard de Lairesse (1640–1711), an influential theorist and advocate of classicism. As John Sunderland has suggested, this most important project of Mortimer's short life may be regarded both as a manifesto of the primacy of the imagination and, with the inclusion of Rosa and Rosa-inspired subject matter, a mild rebuke to Reynolds's classicism (Sunderland 1988, p. 92).

Executed entirely with the pen, the present drawing represents a heavily muscled, turbaned male figure seated beneath a tree, his head leaning on his hand. The figure and general compositional design are close to those in a drawing recently on the art market, *Four Banditti Resting Under a Tree* (Sotheby's, London, 8 April 1998, lot 6), which Mortimer adapted from an etching by Rosa (Sunderland 1970, p. 520, fig. 40; Bartsch, XX.283.50). The pose of the figure in the Morgan drawing recalls that of Dürer's engraving *Melancholia I* of 1514 (Schoch et al. 2001, no. 71), a popular and widely disseminated print that Mortimer could have seen in the study collection of the Royal Academy or in any number of private collections in London. He may have intentionally invoked the Renaissance master's model inasmuch as it was recognized as a symbol of creative genius.

KS

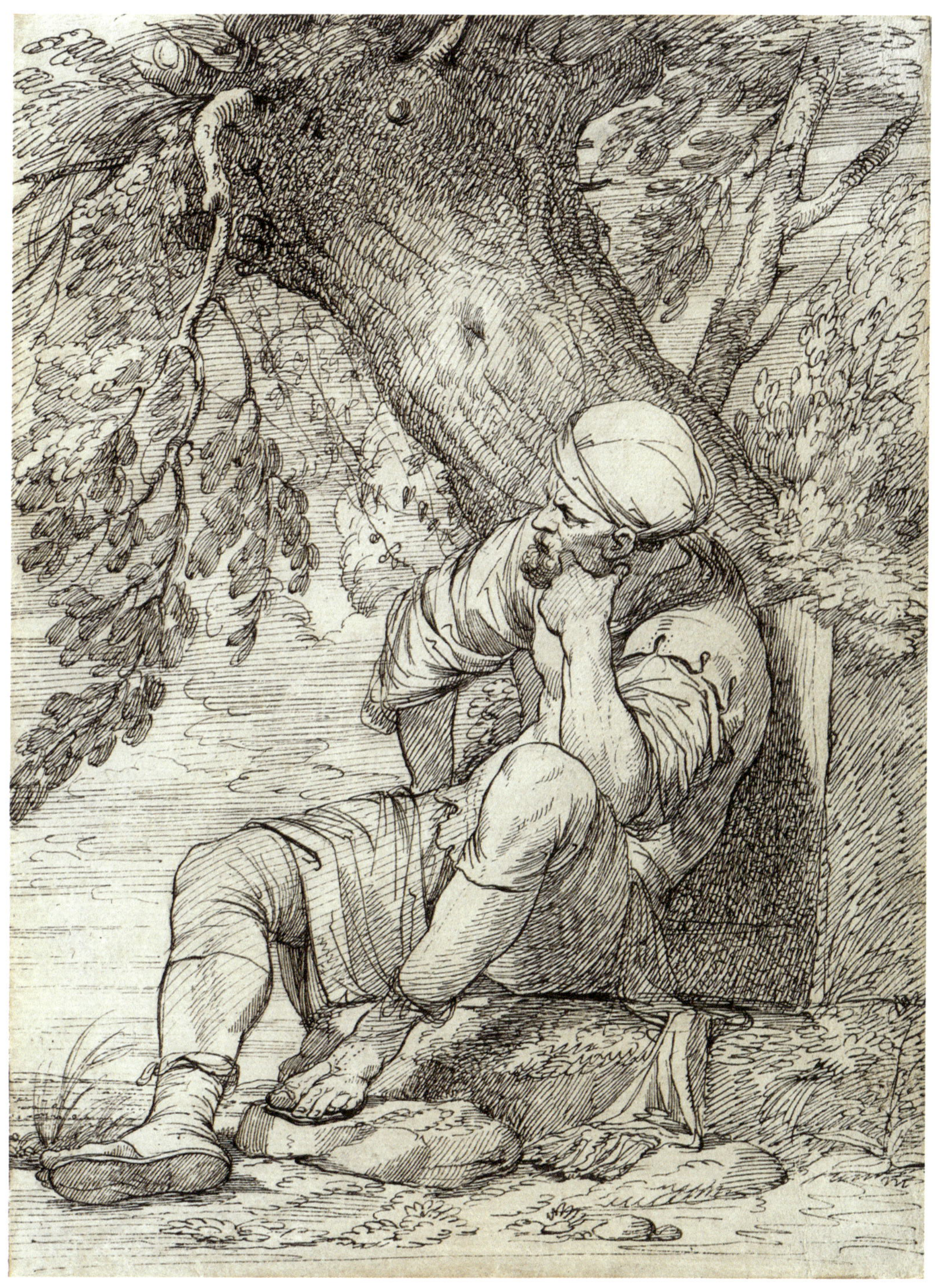

JOHN ROBERT COZENS British, London 1752–1797 London

# 18. *View from Mirabella in the Euganean Hills, near Padua*

Watercolor over graphite; lined. 10 1/16 × 14 3/4 inches (256 × 374 mm).

PROVENANCE: Henry Harris, Esq., London, 1921 (according to Agnew's, London, files); Thomas Agnew & Sons, London, 1937 (their label on frame backing, inventory number 8955); through whom acquired by Norman D. Newall, Esq. (1888–1952), Newbrough, Northumberland, 1937; his sale, Christie's, London, 13 December 1979, lot 24; from which acquired by Ian Woodner (1903–1990), New York (his label on frame backing, inventory number WWA-88); his sale, Christie's, London, 9 July 1991, lot 89; private collection, U.K.; acquired from Andrew Clayton-Payne Ltd., London.

BIBLIOGRAPHY: Bell and Girtin 1935, no. 217; Sotheby's 1973, under lot 23; Clayton-Payne 2007, pp. 17–19.

EXHIBITIONS: London 1937, no. 152; Manchester 1937, no. 74; Newcastle-upon-Tyne 1953, no. 19.

2003.47

John Robert Cozens was the son and pupil of Alexander Cozens, a founder of the British landscape school and a member of the first generation of artists to execute finished landscapes in watercolor. Working at a time when artists were shifting from purely topographical depictions to designs that conveyed an emotional response to their subject, John Robert created some of the first British landscapes infused with poetry.

Cozens made his second sojourn in Italy in 1782–83, traveling with the young antiquarian William Beckford (1760–1844), for whom he filled seven sketchbooks recording the classical sites popular with travelers on the Grand Tour. In June 1782 he made four drawings in the Euganean Hills, a picturesque region in the Veneto, southwest of Padua (Sotheby's 1973, nos. 19, 22, 23, 24), including the preparatory study for the present drawing (Fig. 1).

This sheet is Cozens's only known finished watercolor of the composition. According to his inscription on the preliminary sketch, it records a view from Mirabella, the villa of Count Francesco Algarotti (1712–1764), where the entourage had stopped on its way to Rome. Tucked into the hillside at left is the Benedictine abbey of Santa Maria di Praglia. In executing the finished watercolor, Cozens closely followed the preliminary sketch with a few significant changes. He deepened the valley and emphasized the rhythmic curves of its open spaces, employing subtle tonal shifts to suggest the rise and fall of the undulating terrain and to define broad areas of sunlight and shade. At right he added a plume of vapor, a possible allusion to the region's volcanic origins. Cozens may have seen such a plume because he recorded it in another of the preliminary sketches and included it in *The Euganean Hills from the Walls of Padua,* the finished drawing after that sketch, in the National Gallery of Scotland, Edinburgh (Sotheby's 1973, no. 19; Sloan 1986, pl. 156).

In a letter to Lady Hamilton dated 19 June 1782, William Beckford described the view from Mirabella recorded so poetically by Cozens's drawing: "Evening drawing on and the breeze blowing cool from the distant Adriatic, I reclin'd on a slope and turned my eyes anxiously towards Venice, then on some little field . . . hemmed in by Chestnuts in blossom, and then, to a Mountain crowned by a circular grove of Fir and Cypress" (Benjamin 1910, p. 155).

KS

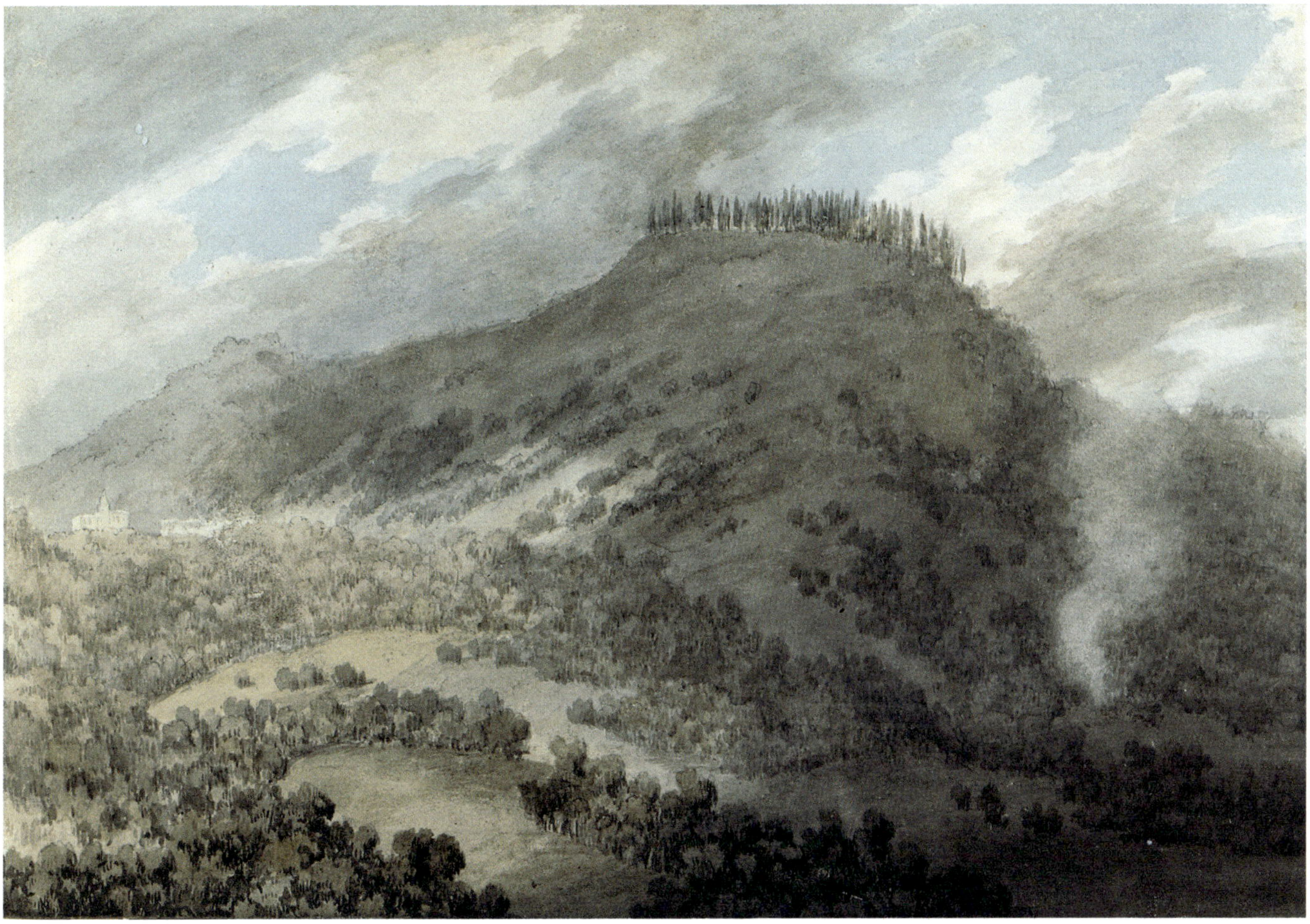

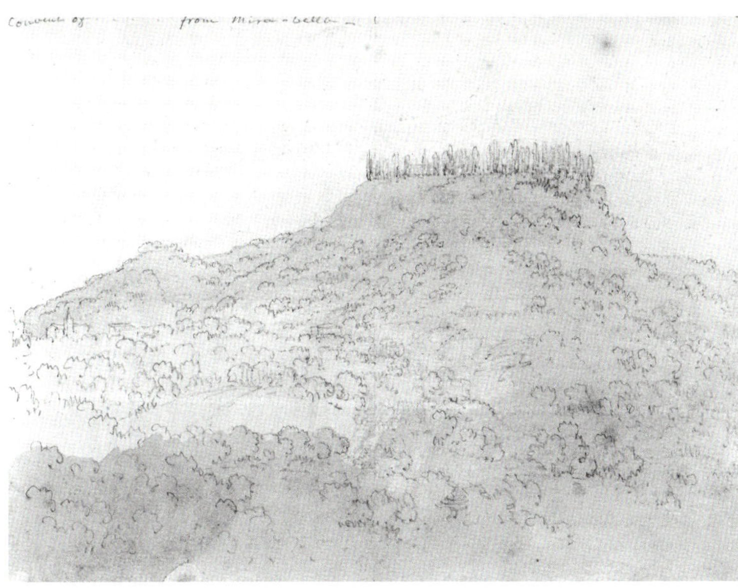


Fig. 1. John Robert Cozens, *Convent of . . . from Mira-bella* (The Whitworth Art Gallery, Manchester)

JOHN ROBERT COZENS British, London 1752–1797 London

# 19. *Mountain Landscape*

Watercolor over graphite. 14 5/16 × 19 15/16 inches (363 × 506 mm).

Inscribed on verso at center in graphite, *from the summit of a mountain / A Cozens*, in a different hand at lower right, *Lay down on 19¾ × 14⅛ Sight*.

WATERMARK: II Taylor; close to Heawood 3441.

PROVENANCE: Private collection, Yorkshire (according to Christie's, London, auction catalogue, 6 June 2002); Christie's, London, 6 June 2002, lot 12; acquired from C. G. Boerner Limited, London.

2002.66

The present drawing is viewed from a great height across a range of mountains to a broad plain and distant mountains on the horizon. The top of a cloud layer in the middle ground at left gives some indication of the altitude. The foreground plane is defined by a broad, bowl-shaped precipice with a tiny human figure barely visible at left, emphasizing the immense scale of the landscape. The barren, rocky terrain is evoked in a mass of individual daubs of the brush in closely chromatic tones of blue, green, and gray. The prospect is of a type that would have appealed to Cozens, recalling his studies of rock faces from when he was a student of his father, Alexander Cozens.

The drawing may represent a view in Switzerland, possibly looking south from the Dolomites into Italy across the Po Valley. Cozens traveled through Switzerland on his first sojourn in Italy in 1776–79 in the company of his patron, the connoisseur Richard Payne Knight, for whom he executed fifty-seven almost monochromatic Swiss views, many of which he used for later, more finished works. As was his practice, Cozens would have executed this drawing in his studio from graphite sketches made on the spot, which have not been identified. Kim Sloan has agreed that the drawing is very close to Cozens and may conceivably be by him, although she observed that the sheet is unusual in Cozens's oeuvre because nothing directly comparable is known. She pointed out that Cozens's last dated work is from 1792 and that he fell ill the following year—an observation difficult to reconcile with the watermark dated 1797 (communication with the author, 19 October 2006 and 6 February 2007). This suggests that either there existed a yet undiscovered pre-1797 II Taylor watermark, or that the drawing is by a yet unidentified close follower of Cozens, or most likely, that Cozens was still able to work during the last years of his life, despite his illness.

The drawing's palette of cool blues, greens, and grays evokes the tinted topographical works of Cozens's mid-eighteenth-century predecessors. But he moves beyond them by using tone to define form and represent light and shadow. Cozens was one of the first British artists to use watercolor in this way, and his influence on the next generation of artists was profound. His drawings served as teaching tools for, among others, the young J. M. W. Turner (see Nos. 24–25), who copied them in the informal sketching club in London run by Dr. Thomas Monro, an early collector of Cozens's work.

KS

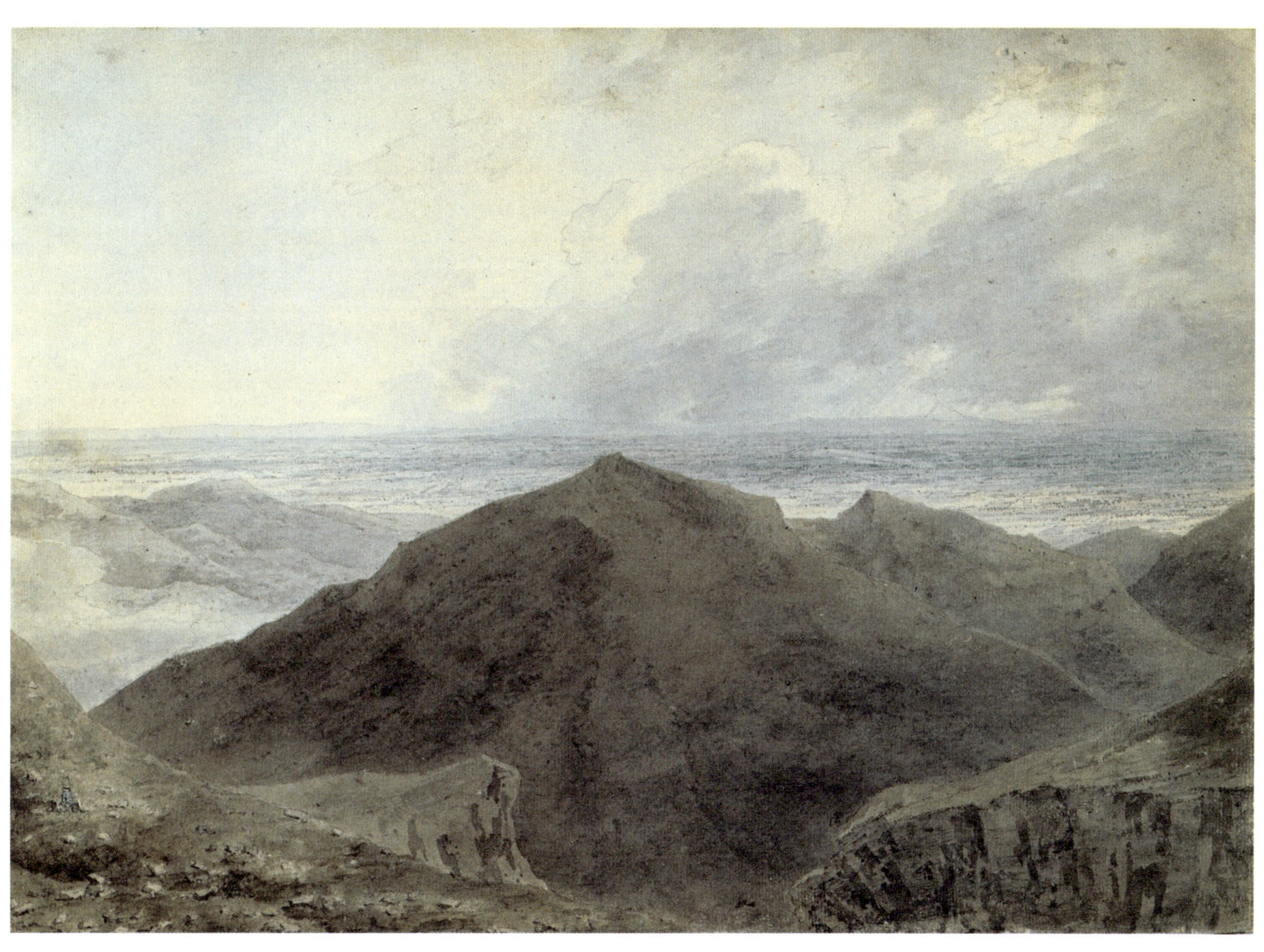

THOMAS DANIELL British, Chertney 1749–1840 London
WILLIAM DANIELL British, [location unknown] 1769–1837 London

# 20. *The Purana Qila, Delhi*

Watercolor over graphite; laid down on old mount. 17 7/16 × 24 1/4 inches (443 × 614 mm).

Inscribed on old mount beneath drawing at center in pen and black ink, *Part of the FORT built by the EMPEROR SHERE SHAH . DEHLI .* [sic].

PROVENANCE: The Bromley-Davenport family, Capesthorne Hall, Cheshire; Gooden & Fox, London, 1951; acquired by Sir John Burder for the Peninsular and Oriental Steam Navigation Company (P & O) Collection, London; its sale, Christie's, London, 24 September 1996, lot 52; acquired from Andrew Clayton-Payne Ltd., London.

BIBLIOGRAPHY: Archer 1980, no. 38; Clayton-Payne 2007, pp. 39–41.

EXHIBITIONS: London 1960, no. 33; London 1974, no. 7.

Purchased on the Sunny Crawford von Bülow Fund in honor of Sir Paul Getty.

2003.27.

Thomas Daniell and his nephew William Daniell were members of a family of painters and printmakers. Thomas apprenticed with a coach painter, then entered the Royal Academy Schools in 1773, exhibiting topographical and architectural landscapes and flower subjects between 1774 and 1784. William trained with his uncle before the pair set out for India in 1785. They were among the first British artists to travel and work in the subcontinent. Often following the route of colonizing British troops, the Daniells traveled to regions never before visited by artist-travelers (Almeida and Gilpin 2005, p. 183). During nearly a decade in India they made watercolor drawings of picturesque sites for eventual publication in the burgeoning market in illustrated travel books. Upon their return they published *Oriental Scenery* (London, 1795–1808), an epic work issued in six volumes and comprising 144 color plates. The most extensive publication to date on the subject, *Oriental Scenery* was immensely popular and widely influential. As Mildred Archer observed, it not only created a vogue in Britain for Indian-inspired architecture and decorative arts, it "formed a popular vision in Britain of a romantic and picturesque India that to some extent persists" (Archer 1996).

This drawing is a study for Thomas Daniell's aquatint engraving entitled *The Western Entrance of Shere Shah's Fort, Delhi*, which appeared as plate 13 in the first volume of *Oriental Scenery*, published March 1796. The Daniells visited the northern Indian city between 16 February and 6 March 1789, the first British artists to record its sites. The drawing represents a view of the western gate of the sixteenth-century fort (also known as the Purana Qila) established by the second Mughal emperor, Humayun, and completed by his successor, the Afghan usurper Sher Shah Sur. Daniell, who favored the realism of Dutch seventeenth-century landscape over the conventions of the Claudean ideal landscape (Almeida and Gilpin 2005, p. 184), faithfully represented the red and yellow sandstone and white marble of the fort's massive gate, which stands largely unchanged today. In a nod to prevailing taste for the work of the so-called English Claude, Richard Wilson (see No. 14), Daniell imagined a hillier foreground dominated by a ruin whose brooding presence contrasts with the clarity of the fort. KS

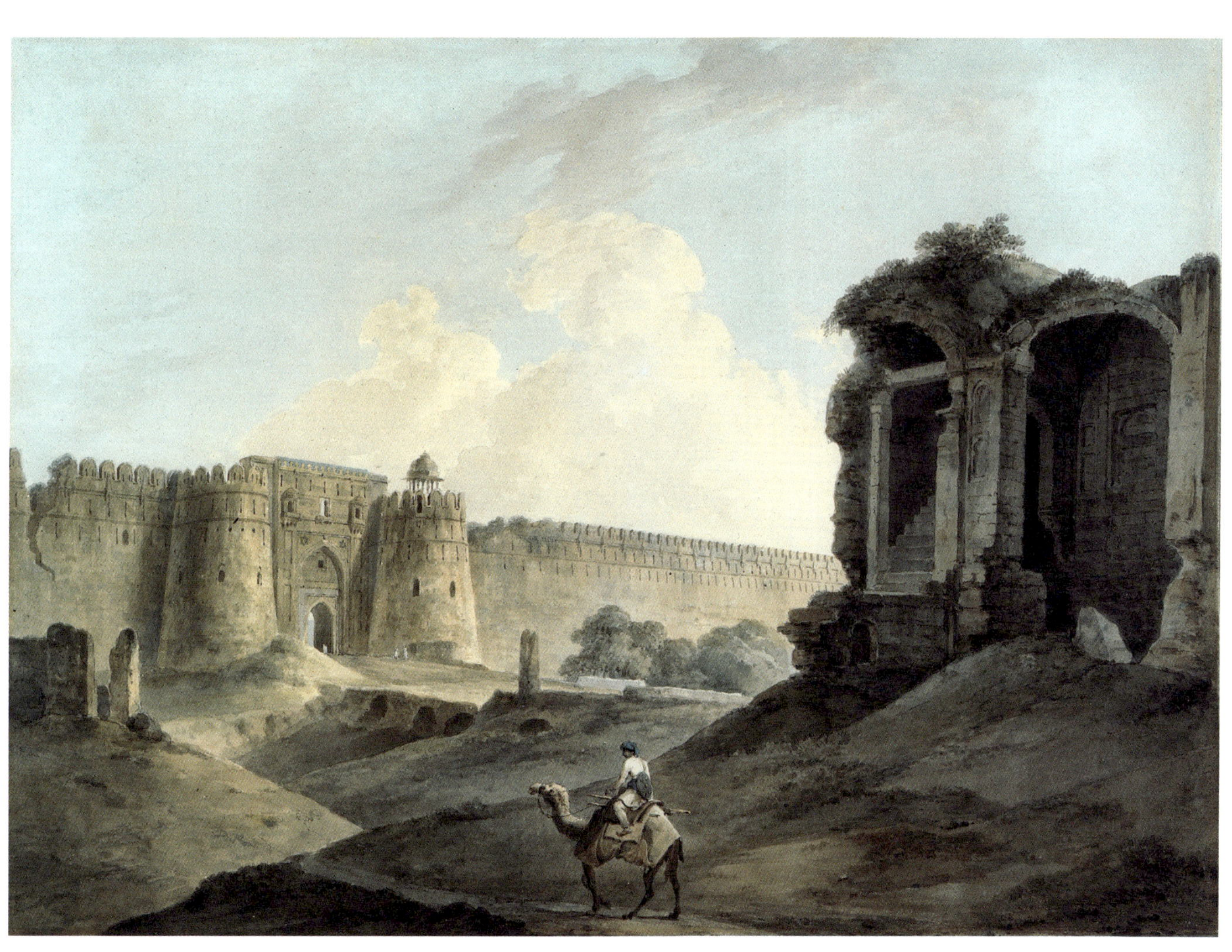

RICHARD WESTALL British, Hertford 1765–1836 London

# 21. *Satan Calling His Spirits from the Fiery Lake*

Watercolor over graphite on wove paper; mounted to card. 22⅜ × 15⅜ inches (570 × 392 mm).

Inscribed on verso of mount at lower left in pen and black ink, *pr[oper]ty of / Nicholas Lanes – Powers [Powell?]*.

PROVENANCE: Possibly Sir Gregory Osborne Page Turner, Oxfordshire; possibly his sale, Phillips, London, 24–26 June 1815; private collection; acquired from Andrew Clayton-Payne Ltd., London.

EXHIBITION: London 1814, no. 274, p. 17.

Purchased on the Sunny Crawford von Bülow Fund in honor of Sir Paul Getty.

2003.13

Following an apprenticeship with the heraldic engraver John Thompson, Westall exhibited his first work at the Royal Academy in 1784 and entered the Royal Academy Schools the following year. He worked mostly in watercolor—a relative rarity at the time—and was one of the first artists whose watercolors were considered by reviewers to rival oil paintings (London and Manchester 2005, p. 15). Elected to the Royal Academy in 1794, he became known for his prolific output of highly finished designs for engraved illustrations to the Bible and the works of Shakespeare and Milton as well as those of the leading poets and authors of the day, including Lord Byron, William Cowper, and Sir Walter Scott. During the last nine years of Westall's life, he gave drawing lessons to the young princess Victoria, the future queen.

The present drawing is the study for the plate, dated 4 June 1794, opposite page 15 of *The Works of John Milton* (John and Josiah Boydell, London, 1794–97). It represents a fair-haired, muscular Satan, with Beelzebub beside him, his broad wings extending beyond the borders of the design. The image conflates several passages from Book I of *Paradise Lost,* in which Satan addresses the fallen angels: . . . *on the beach / Of that inflamed sea he stood, and call'd / His legions, angels forms . . . He call'd so loud, that all the hollow Deep / Of Hell resounded. . . .* (ll. 299–301; 314–15).

Westall depicted Satan in a heroic pose against a black background, foreshortening the figure to emphasize the dramatic tension of the scene. With the point of the brush he used delicate cross- and parallel hatching to define the contours of the face and the muscles of the neck, torso, and thighs. To suggest the fiery sea at lower left, he layered transparent washes in tones of red, ocher, tan, and gray.

The depiction of Satan as hero was common in the late eighteenth century, particularly among artists illustrating *Paradise Lost;* for them the fallen angel had become a symbol of revolutionary rebellion. Other examples of the period include *Satan Starting at the Touch of Ithuriel's Lance* by Henry Fuseli (1741–1825), a painting of 1780 (Staatsgalerie, Stuttgart; London 2006, no. 37), and *Satan and His Legions Hurling Defiance Toward the Vault of Heaven,* an etching of about 1792–95 by James Barry (1741–1806; London 2006, no. 46).

KS

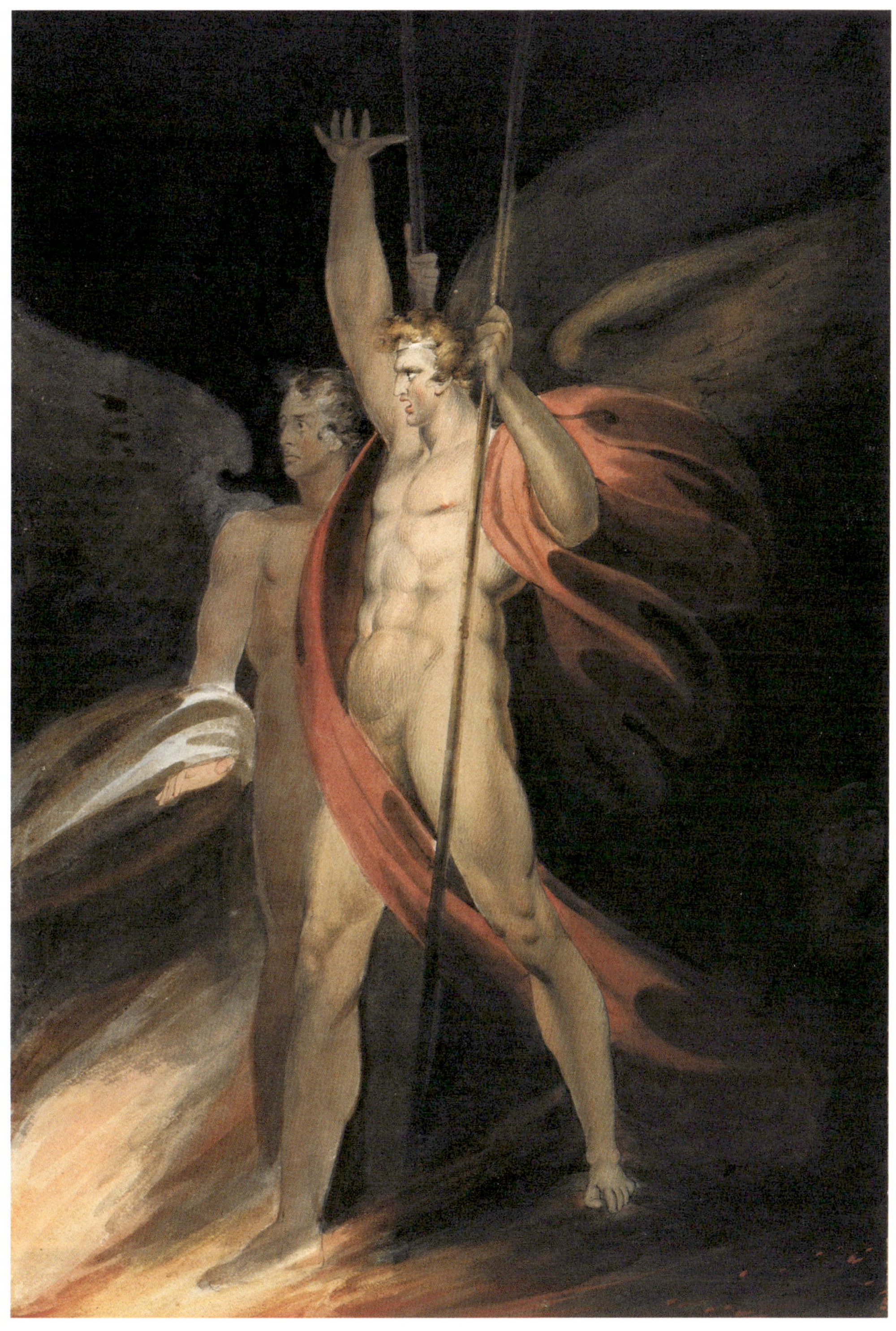

# 22. *A Scene from Milton's* Paradise Regained, 1804

Brush and gray wash over graphite. 12½ × 17⁷⁄₁₆ inches (318 × 444 mm).

Inscribed by the artist on verso at center, in pen and brown ink, *Subject / Either tropick now / Gan thunder: At both ends of Heaven, the clouds, / From many a horrid rift abortive, pour'd / Fierce rain with Lightning mixd. Water with fire / In Ruin reconcil'd - / Milton. / Presidt. JS. Cotman, - W Havell. J Powell. P S Munn, T Webster. J Hayward. J Varley / Mr Crystal. – Visitor – Mr Stevens / May 3rd. Thursday. / 1804.*; above this, in graphite in a different hand, *He gave them hail-stones for rain; fire / Mingled with the hail. ran along the ground.*

PROVENANCE: H. D. Hargraves, F.R.S.H.; his sale, Sotheby's, London, 30 March 1983, lot 107; by descent until 2002; sale, Sotheby's, London, 28 March 2002, lot 262; acquired from Thomas Agnew & Sons Ltd., London.

2003.25

Cotman left his native Norwich for London about 1798 and was soon taken up by the patron and teacher Thomas Monro (1759–1833), whose informal drawing salon had nurtured the talents of J. M. W. Turner (see Nos. 24–25) and Thomas Girtin (1775–1802). Cotman began copying the drawings of the older artists, which apparently constituted his only training. A precocious draftsman, he exhibited for the first time at the Royal Academy just two years later. In the summers of 1803–5 he sojourned in Yorkshire, producing a group of watercolors that are astonishing in their sophisticated abstraction and among the most innovative landscapes of his generation.

The present drawing, previously unpublished, was made during this fertile period in Cotman's career. An imaginary view, it was inspired by a passage from John Milton's *Paradise Regained* (Book IV, ll. 409–13), quoted in the inscription in Cotman's hand on the verso, in which Christ's struggles against Satan are symbolized by fierce storms. Cotman set the scene in a clearing along a riverbank under a brooding, cloud-filled sky, with a single large tree at left and dense foliage at right serving as foreground *repoussoir*. The clouds and foliage are depicted in Cotman's characteristic wash manner of layering closely gradated tone, which serves to abstract his subject and causes the forms almost to bloom across the sheet.

In the middle ground at right stands a group of Italianate buildings and at left are a pyramid and part of an aqueduct. These elements appear in another of Cotman's Milton-inspired drawings of the period, *Towered Cities Please Us Then* (Victoria and Albert Museum, London; London 1982, no. 29), and are thought to have been adapted from J. M. W. Turner's painting *The Fifth Plague of Egypt*, exhibited in London in 1800 (Indianapolis Museum of Art; Wilton 1979, no. P13). Near the center of the composition is a small group of figures gathered along the riverbank. The figure in white robes, probably representing Christ, gestures toward the sky, which clears in the upper right quadrant of the sheet as though in response to the figures' prayerful entreaties.

As we know from Cotman's inscription on the verso, the drawing was executed during a meeting of the Sketching Society in London, a group of artists founded by Thomas Girtin in 1799 and headed by Cotman from 1802 (Wilton 1977, p. 34). At their weekly sessions, the host chose a brief poetic text for the artists to render in a monochrome wash drawing and to complete in the course of the evening. Cotman was host on the evening when this drawing was made, his final documented contact with the group (London 1983). The Morgan preserves another drawing executed during a Sketching Society meeting, Thomas Girtin's *The Eruption of Mount Vesuvius* (1996.147; London 1996–97, no. 51), made in 1799 or 1800.

KS

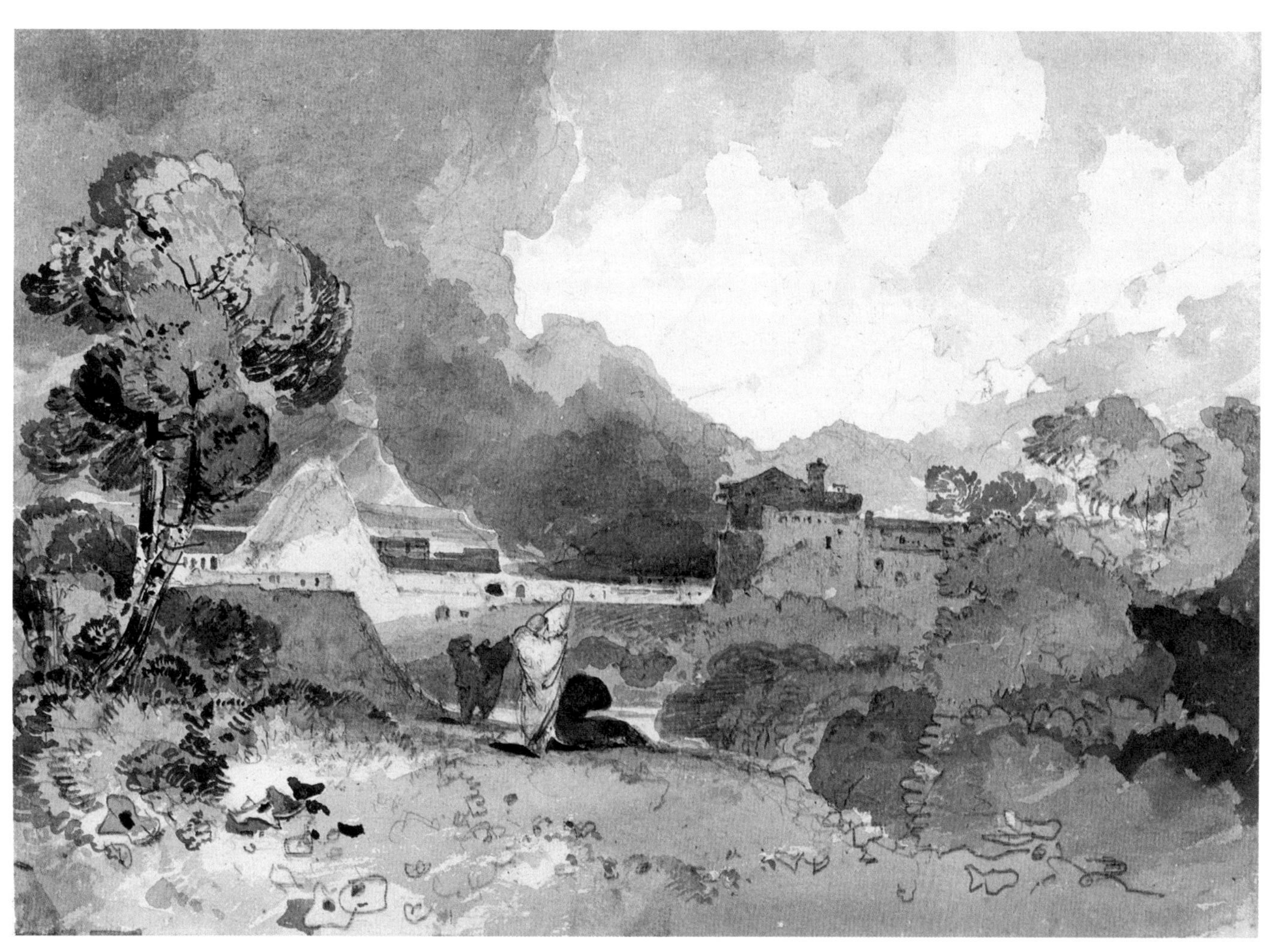

# 23. *The East End of the Bauchon Chapel, Norwich Cathedral,* 1807–8

Watercolor over graphite, on two sheets of tan paper. The original sheet has been extended about 1½ inches (39 mm). 16 13/16 × 10⅞ inches (427 × 275 mm).

Inscribed variously by the artist in graphite with color notations, *Oker . . . Whi . . . Oak*; inscribed by C. F. Bell on old mount in graphite, *East End of the Beauchamp Chapel / 1806–10*.

PROVENANCE: Sir Thomas Barlow (1845–1945); acquired from Artemis Fine Arts Inc., New York.

BIBLIOGRAPHY: *Artemis* 1998, no. 13.

EXHIBITIONS: Manchester 1937, no. 39; New York 1996, no. 30.

1997.15

Although Cotman's work was enthusiastically regarded by connoisseurs and collectors, in 1806 he failed to be elected to London's Society of Painters in Watercolours. Following this disappointment, he returned to his native Norwich, where he established a drawing school and began making watercolors of local subjects, including *The Market Place, Norwich* (Abbot Hall Art Gallery, Kendal; London and elsewhere 1982–83a, no. 57) and *The Cow Tower* (private collection, London and elsewhere 1982–83a, no. 59), both of 1807. One local feature, Norwich Cathedral, seems to have held special interest, for during the years 1807–8 he made at least five drawings of the interior, including the present sheet (see London and elsewhere 1982–83a, nos. 62–65). As his biographer Sydney Kitson observed, these drawings were made at a time when "Cotman was recording architecture with an artist's eye" (Kitson 1937, p. 107).

Cotman had an affinity for architectural subjects, as some of his earliest drawings attest, for example, *The Old College House, Conway* of 1802 (Cecil Higgins Art Gallery, Bedford; London and elsewhere 1982–83a, no. 7). Beginning about 1810 and continuing for over a decade, he devoted himself to making etchings in this genre to be published and sold to clients, among them *Architectural Antiquities of Norfolk* (1812–18) and the widely acclaimed *Architectural Antiquities of Normandy* (1822). His Norwich Cathedral subjects, however, apparently were made for his own pleasure and seem never to have been reproduced as prints (Kitson 1937, p. 134).

The present drawing represents the Bauchon (or Beauchamp) Chapel of Norwich Cathedral, added to the Norman-era cathedral in 1329. Cotman began the drawing with quick notations in graphite to lay out the general contours of the design, with color notes for future reference, adding washes in the studio. Employing a technique characteristic of his drawings of this period, he brushed in layer upon layer of close chromatic tones of gray, taupe, brown, and ocher, with touches of pale green, leaving some areas unpainted to reveal the tan of the paper. In the area to the right of the figure, for example, gradated layers of tone, with clearly defined edges created by the application of a wet brush, produce a mottled effect that convincingly evokes the look of centuries-old weathered stone. The addition of a figure, unique among Cotman's known drawings of cathedral interiors, not only establishes scale but also imbues the work with a finished, pictorial quality lacking in the other examples from this series.

KS

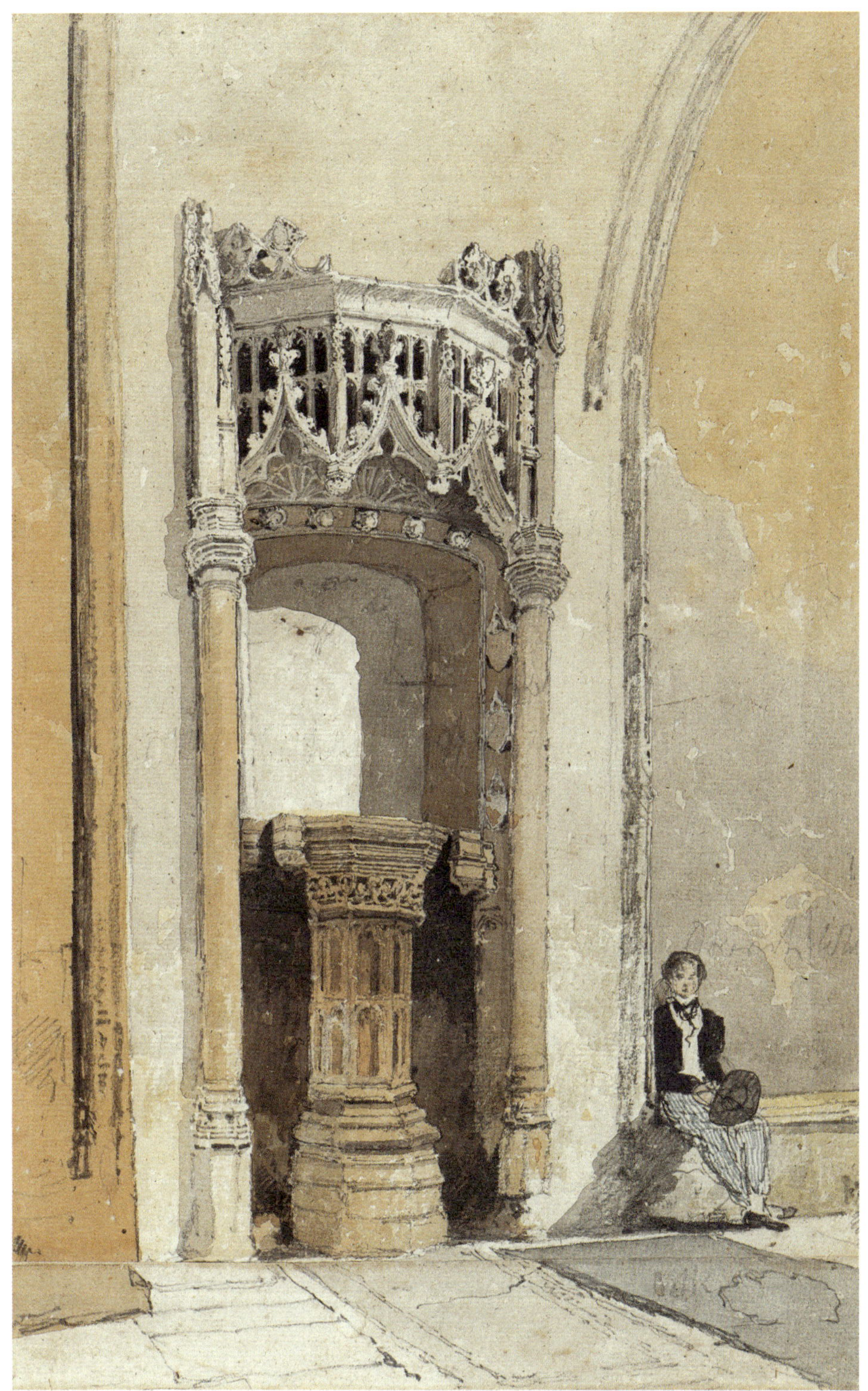

# 24. *View of Crichton Castle,* ca. 1818

Watercolor and scraping out. 6⅜ × 9½ inches (161 × 240 mm).

PROVENANCE: Sir Walter Scott (1771–1832), Abbotsford, Roxburgh, Scotland; by descent to his grandniece Mary Monica Maxwell Scott, 1858; Ralph Brocklebank (1840–1921), Childwall Hall, Lancashire, by 1882; his son, Thomas Brocklebank (died 1919), Heswall Hall, Cheshire, by 1899; his sale, Christie's, London, 8 July 1938, lot 14; bought Rayner MacConnell, London; from whom acquired by John William MacKay, Earl of Inchcape; Mrs. Francis Tompkins; her sale, Sotheby's, London, 13 October 1954, lot 30 (bought Callender); Viscountess Garnock; her sale, Christie's, London, 1 March 1977, lot 144 (withdrawn); Viscountess Garnock; her sale, Christie's, London, 21 November 1978, lot 77 (bought Branson); private collection, U.K.; acquired from Andrew Clayton-Payne Ltd., London.

BIBLIOGRAPHY: Brocklebank 1911, no. 113, repr.; Wilton 1979, no. 1059, p. 425; Edinburgh 1999–2000, under no. 15, p. 81, as whereabouts unknown.

EXHIBITIONS: London 1886, no. 45; London 1899, no. 98a–h.

2006.11

This drawing records a view of Crichton Castle, located in Midlothian, in the rugged landscape of northern Scotland, about ten miles south of Edinburgh. Turner traveled through the area in the fall of 1818, making sketches for a new project commissioned by the Scottish novelist and poet Sir Walter Scott (1771–1832), *The Provincial Antiquities and Picturesque Scenery of Scotland,* a suite of engravings after drawings by Turner and other artists representing Scottish monuments and landscape with text by Scott. Published in London, the suite was issued in parts between 1819 and 1826. The engraving after the present drawing was published in August 1819 and appeared on page 51 of volume 1.

Crichton Castle was begun in the fourteenth century and was the principal residence of James, 3rd Earl of Bothwell, third husband of Mary, Queen of Scots, and in the 1570s that of Francis Stewart, 5th Earl of Bothwell, who added the castle's piazza and courtyard modeled on the Palazzo dei Diamanti in Ferrara, which was celebrated in Sir Walter Scott's poem *Marmion.* The castle still stands in a landscape largely unchanged since Turner's day.

During his Scottish sojourn Turner filled four notebooks with compositional sketches mostly in pencil to be used for his finished drawings for the Scott project. One of these, in his *"Scottish Antiquities" Sketchbook,* records highly detailed views of the castle and surrounding landscape (Tate Gallery, London; Edinburgh 1999–2000, fig. 9, p. 27). He also made nearly abstract color studies of the design: one in his *"Scotland and London" Sketchbook* (Fig. 1), and the other, *Crichton Castle with Rainbow,* in the Yale Center for British Art, New Haven (Edinburgh 1999–2000, no. 16).

In all, Turner produced ten designs for the project. Eight of these, including the present sheet, Sir Walter Scott mounted together in a frame made from an oak tree felled on the grounds of Abbotsford, the poet's final estate (Brocklebank 1911, no. 113). The eight so-called Abbotsford Turners remained together until the group was broken up and sold in 1938.

KS

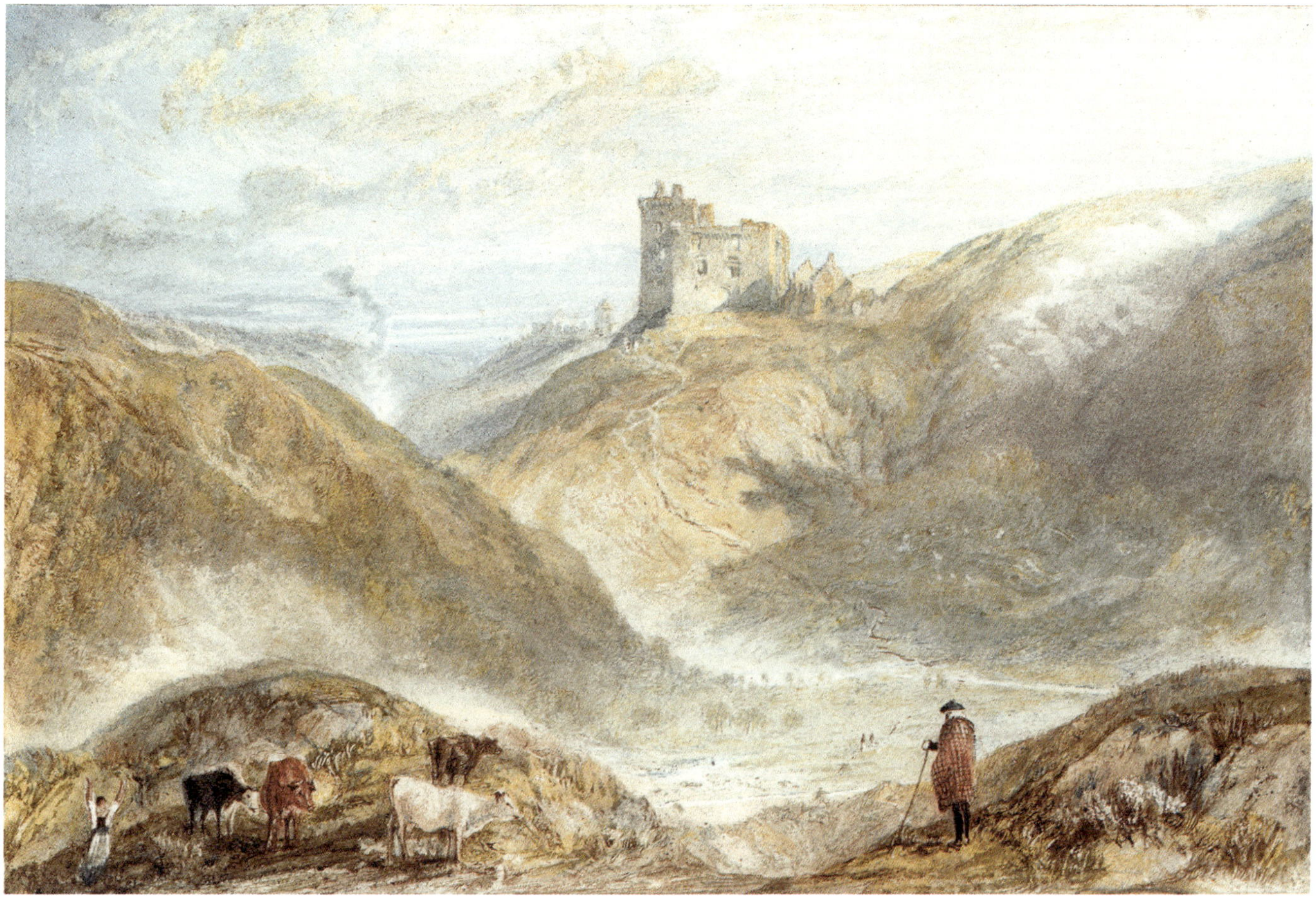

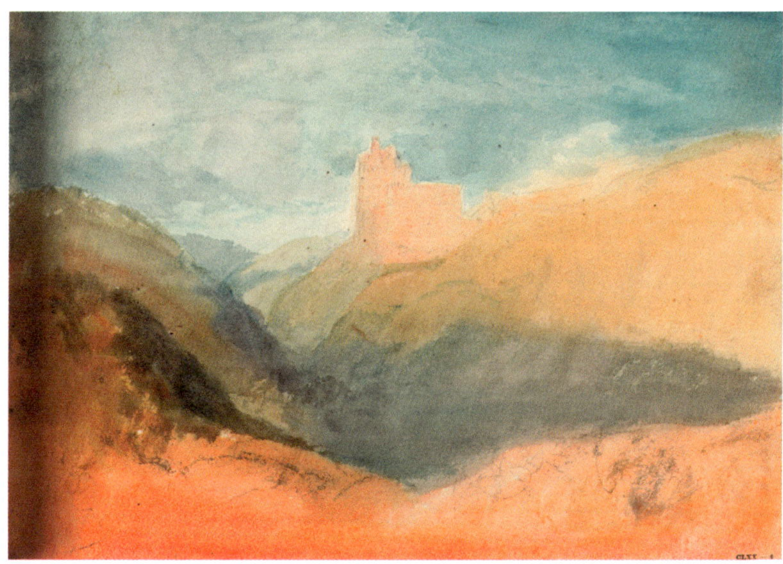

Fig. 1. Joseph Mallord William Turner, *View of Crichton Castle* (Tate Gallery, London)

# 25. *Dartmouth Cove*, 1824–27

Watercolor, point of brush, some gouache, heightened with white gouache. 11 × 15¾ inches (281 × 403 mm).

PROVENANCE: Charles Heath (1785–1848); Benjamin Godfrey Windus (1790–1867), by June 1833; John Heugh, 1874; his sale, London, Christie's, 24 April 1874, lot 93; Thomas Agnew & Sons Ltd., London (according to Wilton 1979); Holbrook Gaskell (1813–1909), Woolton Wood, Liverpool; his sale, London, Christie's, 25 June 1909, lot 233; [Mr.?] King (according to Wilton 1979); Frank Gaskell, 1937 (according to Wilton 1979); by descent to Mr. and Mrs. Ernest Gaskell, 1989; acquired at their sale, London, Sotheby's, 16 November 1989, lot 80, by Leger Galleries, London (later Spink-Leger Pictures; their stamp on frame backing, no. K3 11177), and Thomas Agnew & Sons Ltd., London; from whom acquired.

BIBLIOGRAPHY: Wilton 1979, no. 787; Shanes 1979, no. 4.

EXHIBITIONS: London and Washington 1993, no. 292; New York 2006, no. 62.

Purchased on the Sunny Crawford von Bülow Fund in honor of the 75th anniversary of the Morgan Library and the 50th Anniversary of the Association of Fellows.

2000.1

This drawing belongs to a group of about one hundred of Turner's finest watercolors that were engraved under the title *Picturesque Views in England and Wales* (London, 1824–36), the seminal project of Turner's career. Dated 1824–27, the drawing represents a view of Dartmouth harbor, in Devon on the southwestern coast of England. According to the text accompanying the published engravings, it depicts a sailor's wedding party held on a grassy promontory overlooking the harbor (*Picturesque Views*, part 1, text following no. 3, London, 1827). The view is taken from the east bank of the River Dart, looking south toward the sea. Just visible in the distance to the left of center are the towers of Dartmouth Castle and St. Petrox Church. Turner made at least two preliminary sketches for the present drawing, both in the *Devon Rivers, No. 2 Sketch Book*, which he used on his 1813 sojourn (British Museum, London, no. 133, pp. 53a–54; Shanes 1979, p. 156).

Dartmouth's picturesque landscape was a favorite of draftsmen of the period, who most often represented it from the sea looking inland. One such picture was *Entrance to Dartmouth, Devon*, by William Daniell (1769–1837), published in 1825 with this tribute: "The prospect . . . has no parallel for beauty in the whole range of English scenery" (Daniell 1825, p. 21, plate opposite p. 21). Turner's unconventional view focuses both on the foreground tableau and the hilly landscape at the center of the composition. He made this drawing after his first Italian sojourn, in 1819–20, and it displays his newfound interest in the effects of light and atmosphere. Indeed, the hills dissolving into mist, particularly in the repeating outlines of the headland, bear comparison with his Alpine views. As was his custom at the time, he used a small pointed brush and painted in tiny strokes to create a mosaic-like surface to this work that effectively evokes the shimmering, mist-laden atmosphere of the English coast. It was these qualities in particular—"clouds, including mist and aerial effects"—that Turner's patron John Ruskin singled out for special praise in *Modern Painters* (Cook and Wedderburn 1903–12, vol. 15, p. 75).

KS

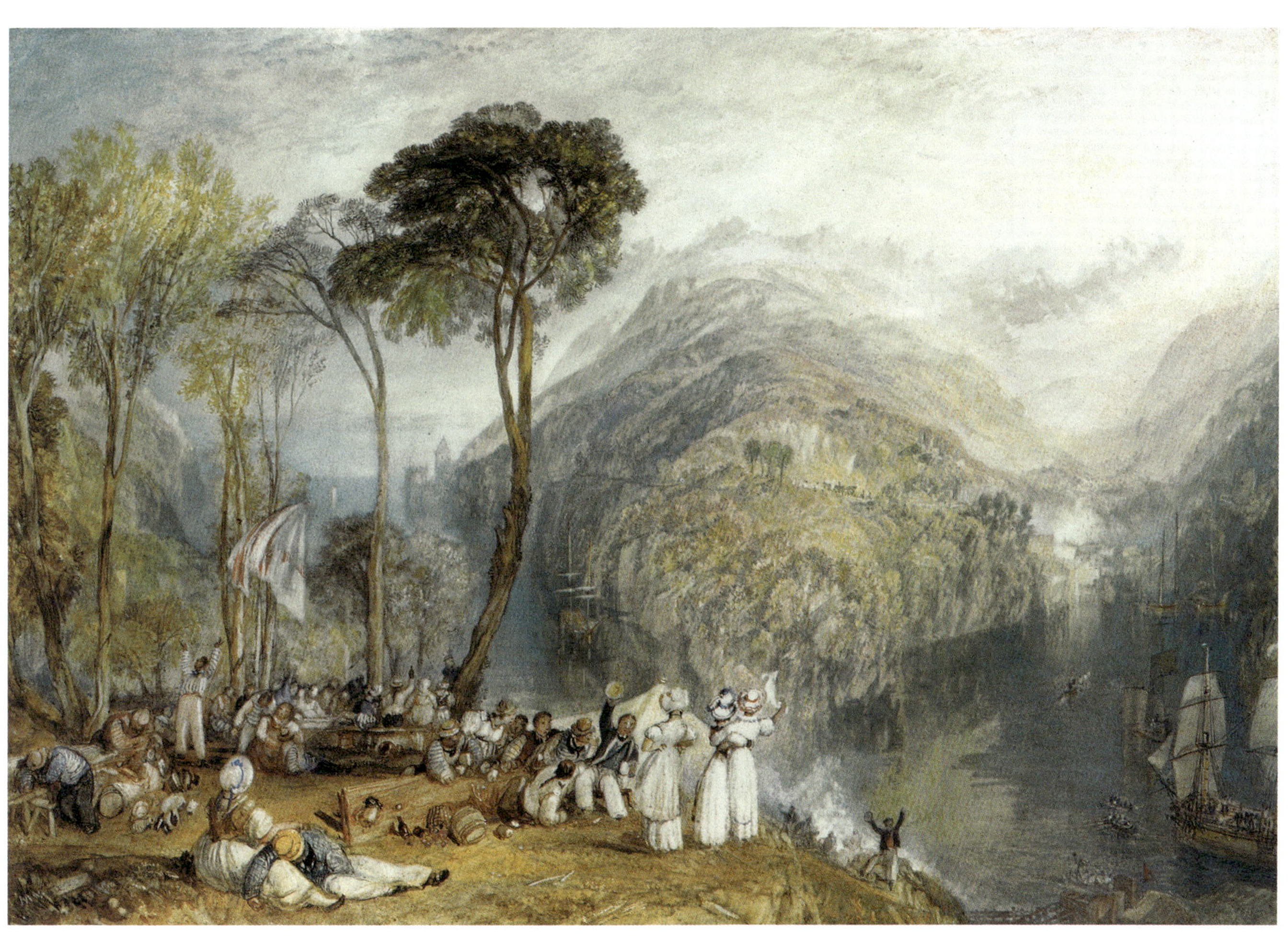

# 26. *The Procession of Cristna*

Watercolor and gouache, heightened with white gouache, with gum arabic, some scratching out, on vellum. 7⅝ × 10⅝ inches (193 × 269 mm).

PROVENANCE: John Gibbons (1777–1851), Bristol; Miss M. Gibbons; her sale, Christie's, London, 29 November 1912, part of lot 76 (unsold); by descent; Mrs. Edward Gibbons (by 1988); sale, Phillips, Knowle, West Milford (U.K.), 10 January 2001 (according to Agnew's, London, files); acquired from Thomas Agnew & Sons Ltd., London.

BIBLIOGRAPHY: Adams 1973, no. 154.

EXHIBITION: Bristol and London 1988–89, no. 99.

2001.18

Born in Ireland of English parents, Danby studied drawing at the Royal Dublin Society before settling in Bristol, in southwestern England, in 1813. He soon distinguished himself, becoming a prominent member of the Bristol school of painters, whose specialty was naturalistic landscapes derived from the native countryside. Despite this tradition, Danby manifested an affinity for the sublime as early as 1819 with his painting *The Upas, or Poison Tree in the Island of Java* (Victoria and Albert, London; Bristol and London 1988–89, no. 18), a large, brooding canvas illustrating a well-known fable. In 1824 he moved to London, where he exhibited regularly at the Royal Academy. A brief sojourn in Norway the following year had a lasting effect on his style, which shifted to imaginative poetic landscapes inspired by literature and the work of the seventeenth-century artists Claude Lorrain and Nicolas Poussin.

This drawing represents an elaborate Indian-style procession of men and elephants through a steep mountain pass. The landscape is comparable to that in Danby's watercolors of about 1825–30 and is thought to have been inspired by the terrain in Norway (see Adams 1973, nos. 116, 117). Although the subject has not been definitively identified, when presented at auction in 1912 the drawing bore the title "The Procession of Krishna," possibly an interpretation of the title on the old frame backing, "The Procession of Crissa." Francis Greenacre (in Bristol and London 1988–89) was the first to give it the present title and to suggest its connection to the artist's epic poem, *Cristna,* which he worked on from about 1820 until 1832, before it went missing in the late 1830s. Today the poem, the subject of which Danby described as "a search for the valley of everlasting life," is known only through letters he wrote to his patron, John Gibbons (Gibbons Family Papers, cited in Bristol and London 1988–89, p. 141).

The drawing is executed on vellum, the smoothness of which combined with gum arabic imparts a subtle sheen to the surface of the work. The technique and choice of media are those of the miniature painter, employing both tiny brushstrokes and broad washes. A similar technique may be observed in other drawings by Danby of the 1820s and 1830s, for example, *A Mountain Lake* of about 1830 (Middlesex, Harrow School; Wilton 1977, pl. 152).

KS

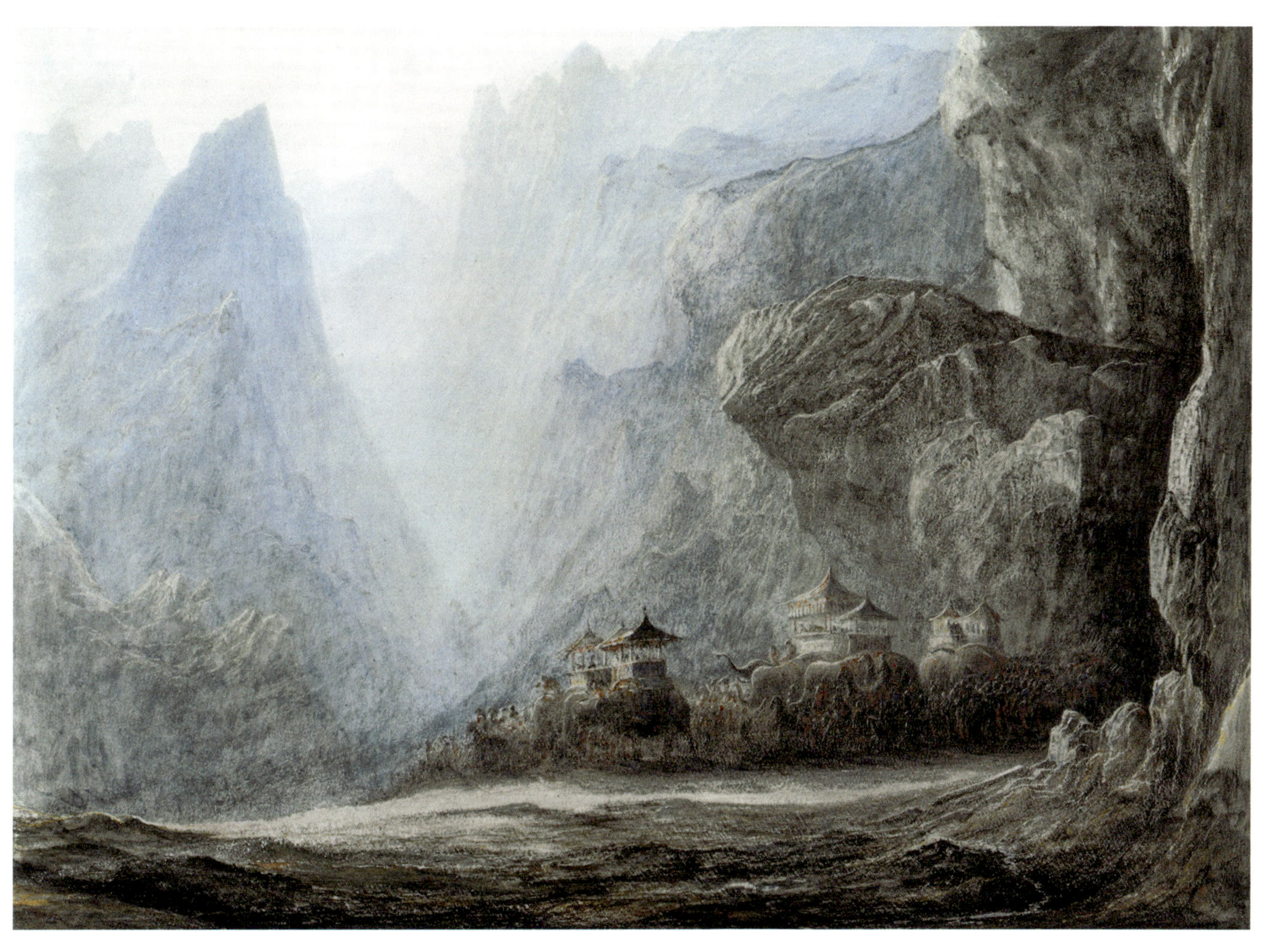

# 27. *The Pont Royal and the Tuileries from the Institut, Paris*

Point of brush and watercolor, over pencil on wove paper. 9¾ × 13⅞ inches (248 × 353 mm).

Signed and dated at lower left, in brown ink, *Thos. Boys 1832*.

PROVENANCE: Anthony Reed, London; private collection, United States (until 1990); acquired from Thomas Agnew & Sons Ltd., London, 2001.

BIBLIOGRAPHY: Roundell 1974, pp. 35, 88, pl. 22.

EXHIBITIONS: Calais 1961; Nottingham and London 1974, no. 27; Louisville 1977, no. 90; San Marino 1986–87, no. 32; London 1990, no. 70.

2001.19

Shotter Boys was apprenticed at age fourteen to George Cooke, one of the most successful engravers of his day. Among the projects being worked on in Cooke's studio at the time was J. M. W. Turner's *Picturesque Views on the Southern Coast of England* (1814–26), no doubt a formidable influence on the young artist whose reputation would be made with his own color-lithographed travel volumes, *Picturesque Architecture in Paris, Ghent, Antwerp, Rouen, etc.* (London, 1839) and *Original Views of London As It Is* (London, 1842). By 1824 Shotter Boys was resident in Paris, remaining there until 1837, when he returned to London. Soon after his arrival in Paris he met and became close friends with Richard Parkes Bonington, whose painting style and color sense he absorbed.

The subject of the present drawing, executed when the artist was twenty-nine, is a view to the east along the Seine in Paris, with the Institut de France at left and the Pont Royal, Musée du Louvre, and Tuileries gardens in the distance. Characteristic of the engraver's art, the drawing is executed with a crispness of detail and a meticulous handling of line typical of Shotter Boys's finished watercolors. This is evident especially in his rendering of the Institut, with its refined treatment of architectural detail, in particular the blue tile roof with cast shadows and the carefully described brickwork of the chimneys. His debt to Bonington may be discerned in the bright spots of intense pure color—the deep reds and rich blues of the figures' cloaks—and in the atmospheric treatment of the billowing clouds whose form balances that of the Institut.

Shotter Boys prepared this drawing with a pencil sketch now in the National Gallery of Canada, Ottawa (Roundell 1974, pl. 21), differing from the finished drawing only in small compositional details.

The Institut viewed from the west was the subject of a watercolor by Shotter Boys dated 1830, now in the Yale Center for British Art, New Haven (Roundell 1974, pl. 15). Although the Yale drawing is composed as a vertical design, the Institut dominates half of the sheet just as it does in the Morgan drawing. A further drawing of the Institut was the model for a color lithograph published as plate 23 in Shotter Boys's *Picturesque Architecture*.

KS

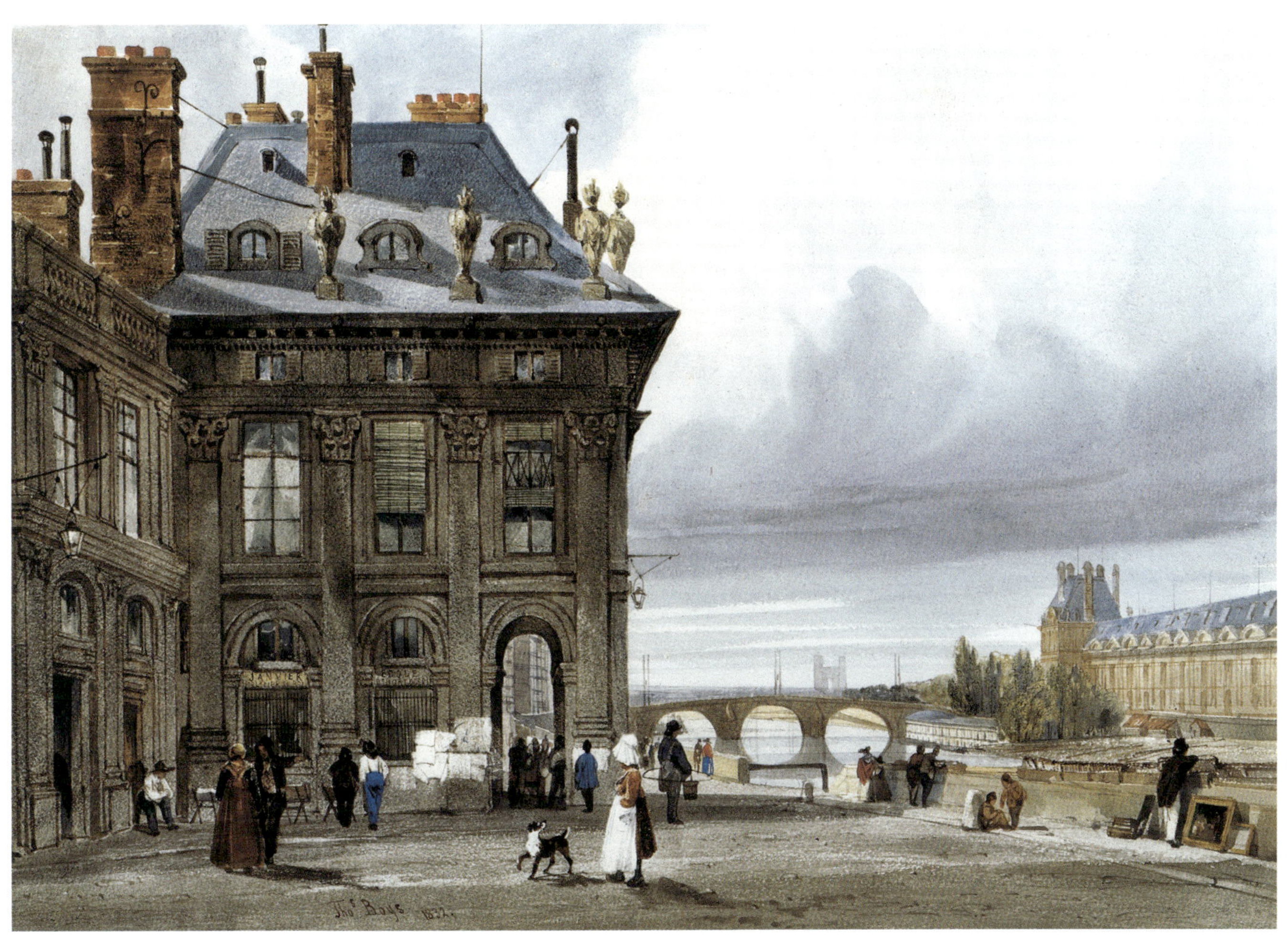

DAVID ROBERTS British, Stockbridge (near Edinburgh) 1796–1864 London

# 28. *Cairo, Looking West,* 1839

Watercolor and gouache over graphite; lined. 13½ × 21¼ inches (341 × 540 mm).

Signed, at lower left, in watercolor, *David Roberts R.A.*, and dated above, in graphite, *Cairo Jany 19th 1839.*; at lower right, in a different hand, in graphite, *El Iuaq[. . .].*

PROVENANCE: The artist's studio sale, Christie's, London, 13 and 15 May 1865, lot 73; from which acquired by Thomas Agnew & Sons Ltd., London; Sir John Pender (1816–1896), London, Glasgow, and Manchester, acquired in 1865; his estate sale, Christie's, London, 29 and 31 May 1897, lot 230; from which acquired by Thomas Agnew & Sons Ltd., London; Rt. Hon. John Frederick Cheetham (1835–1916), Stalybridge; sale, Somerset, early 1950s; private collection, Somerset, from the 1950s; sale, Lawrence's of Crewkerne, Somerset, 17–20 October 2006, lot 1448; acquired from Andrew Clayton-Payne Ltd., London.

BIBLIOGRAPHY: London 1894, no 243; Matyjasczkiewicz and Llewellyn (forthcoming).

2007.1

Roberts began his career as a designer and decorator for the theater in Scotland and London but left this profession in 1830 to paint full time. His early paintings of European architectural and topographical views were well received and exhibited at the Royal Academy. During the 1830s, he traveled in Europe and the Near East, seeking out exotic locations and subjects. He was one of the first British artists to go to Spain (1832–33), and the first artist to journey independently around Egypt, the Sinai, and the eastern Mediterranean (1838–39; Llewellyn 1996, p. 463). The numerous sketches and watercolors he made during this journey provided him with an abundant cache of city views, figure studies, and architectural details to incorporate into oil paintings upon his return to Britain. Roberts's fascination with the East was the defining feature of his artistic career, and the popularity of his works derived in part from the fact that they represented biblical locales (Llewellyn in London 1986, p. 72). His views of Near Eastern landscapes, cities, and monuments were widely dispersed in a six-volume series of lithographic prints after his drawings, published as *The Holy Land: Syria, Idumea, Arabia, Egypt & Nubia* by F. G. Moon between 1842 and 1849.

According to Briony Llewellyn, who has made an extensive study of this sheet, Roberts executed this sweeping view of Cairo during his six-week stay in the city from December 1838 to February 1839. In his journal, he noted on 18 January: "Made three sketches of parts of the Town seen from the mounds outside the walls." (Ballantine 1866, p. 109). The date inscribed on this watercolor indicates that he elaborated on his initial observations the following day, presumably rearranging the scene into a pleasing composition and adding color to organize the city in alternating bands of dark and light wash. Several monuments are clearly identifiable, such as the fourteenth-century Al-Aqsunqur Mosque (later known as the Blue Mosque) in the right foreground and the pyramids in the far distance (Caroline Williams, conversation with the author, 16 March 2007). Yet some details, such as the minaret of the Al-Aqsunqur, have been moved to retain the picturesque qualities of the composition. Roberts's main interest in panoramic vistas was not to chronicle minute details or passing atmospheric effects; rather, as John Ruskin observed in his *Praeterita*, he attempted to capture the "constant aspect of any place" (Cook and Wedderburn 1903–12, 35, p. 404).

Louis Haghe reproduced this view of the city in lithograph (Roberts 1842–49, vol. 1, p. 239) but left out the strong contrast between the dark blue shadows and the golden tones that Roberts juxtaposed in the watercolor to brilliant effect. Llewellyn has identified two other similarly sized watercolor studies of Cairo from an elevated viewpoint: one, dated eight days later, is in the Victoria and Albert Museum (acc. no. SD873; Washington 1995, pl. 73), and another general view of the city is in a private collection (whereabouts unknown; photograph with B. Llewellyn in 2007). ABB

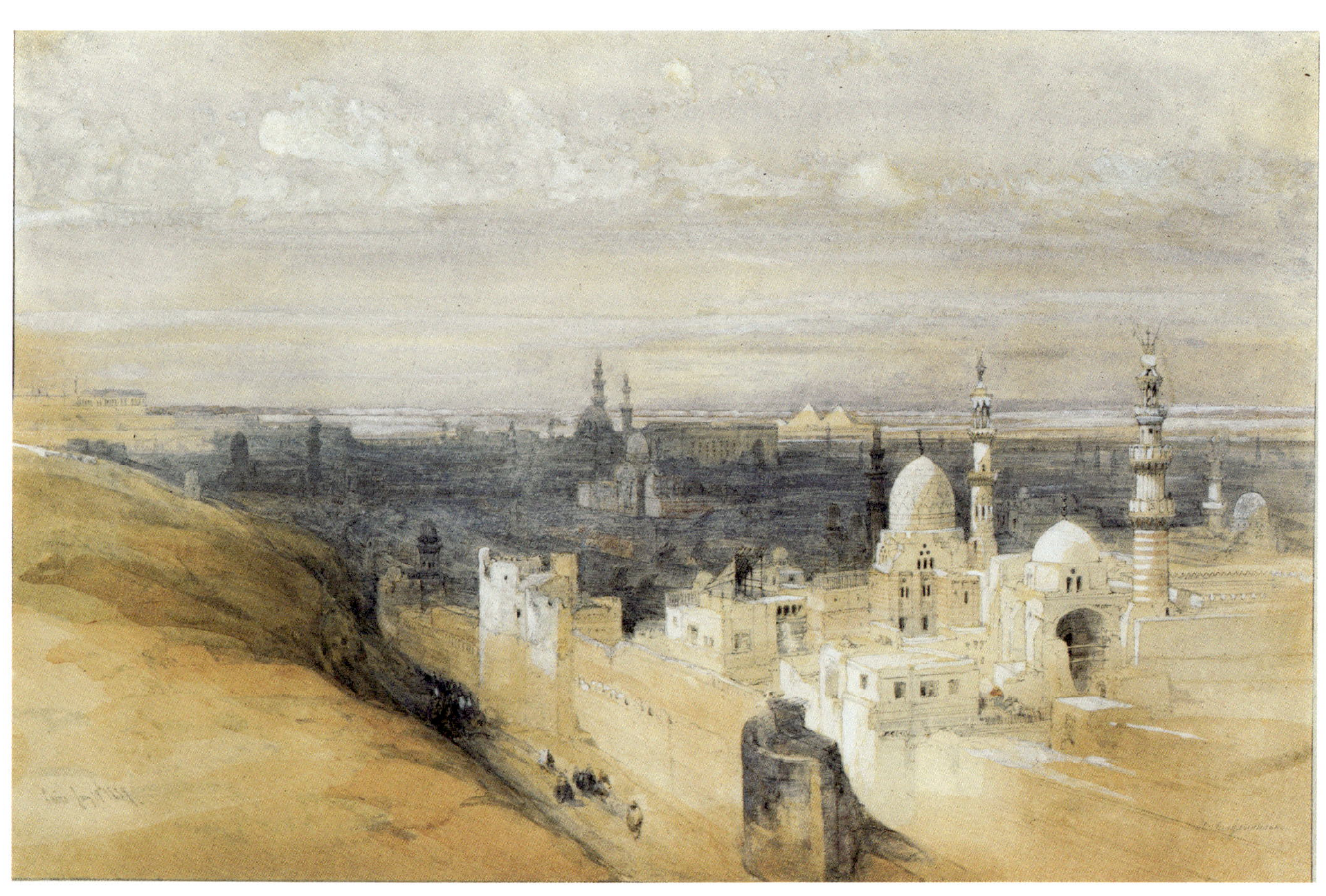

GEORGE RICHMOND British, London 1809–1896 London

# 29. *Recumbent Youth Startled by an Owl,* ca. 1829–30

Pen and brown and black ink, brown wash, blue watercolor, over black chalk. 11¼ × 14⅜ inches (285 × 365 mm).

WATERMARK: Whatman / Turkey Mill / 1827.

PROVENANCE: Acquired from Thomas Agnew & Sons Ltd., London.

EXHIBITION: London 2001, no. 9, pl. VII, introduction (unpaginated), and under no. 41.

2001.85

The son of the portrait-miniaturist Thomas Richmond, George Richmond built a highly successful career as a portraitist, representing in drawings and paintings some of the most famous people of his day. A brilliant draftsman, he entered the Royal Academy Schools in 1824, one of the youngest artists then enrolled, and exhibited his first work, *Abel the Shepherd,* six months later (Tate Gallery, London; Lister 1981, fig. 18). The following year he met William Blake (1757–1827) and joined the group of artists around Blake that included Samuel Palmer (see No. 30) and Edward Calvert. Known as The Ancients for their devotion to the art and literature of the past, they worked in the village of Shoreham in Kent during the middle to late 1820s, studying and debating the works of Virgil, Shakespeare, and Milton and drawing after nature in the countryside they considered their "native English wilderness" (London 2001). More so than did Palmer, whose métier was landscape, Richmond, responding early to Blake's reverence for Michelangelo, expressed himself in the figure.

In this apparently allegorical work, which Susan Sloman dates about 1829–30 (London 2001), a nude male figure reclines on a rush mat, his right hand pointing to a book that lies open on the floor next to an oil lamp. The figure turns away from his reading, startled by an owl at the window. Although the drawing has not been connected to a painting or print, its meaning, while unclear, may be related to Richmond's choice of model for the figure: that of the fourth-century Athenian philosopher Diogenes, the central figure in Raphael's *School of Athens* fresco in the Vatican, who abandons worldly pleasures in the pursuit of truth (London 2001).

In creating this drawing, Richmond, who had not yet been to Italy, borrowed elements from works by Michelangelo he apparently saw in prints: the pointing gesture of the right arm recalls that of God the Father in the Sistine Chapel ceiling fresco *The Creation of Adam,* and the unfinished left arm is adapted from the *David.* For the head and face, Richmond looked to his close friend Samuel Palmer, whose likeness he represented on numerous occasions. In a delicate pencil drawing in the National Portrait Gallery, London, dated about 1829 (Ormond 1973, vol. 2, fig. 698), the high forehead and depiction of the hair are particularly close to the features of the present drawing. The vigorous pen line is employed in other works of the period, for example, *The Blessed Valley* of 1829 (private collection, England; Lister 1981, fig. 22).

KS

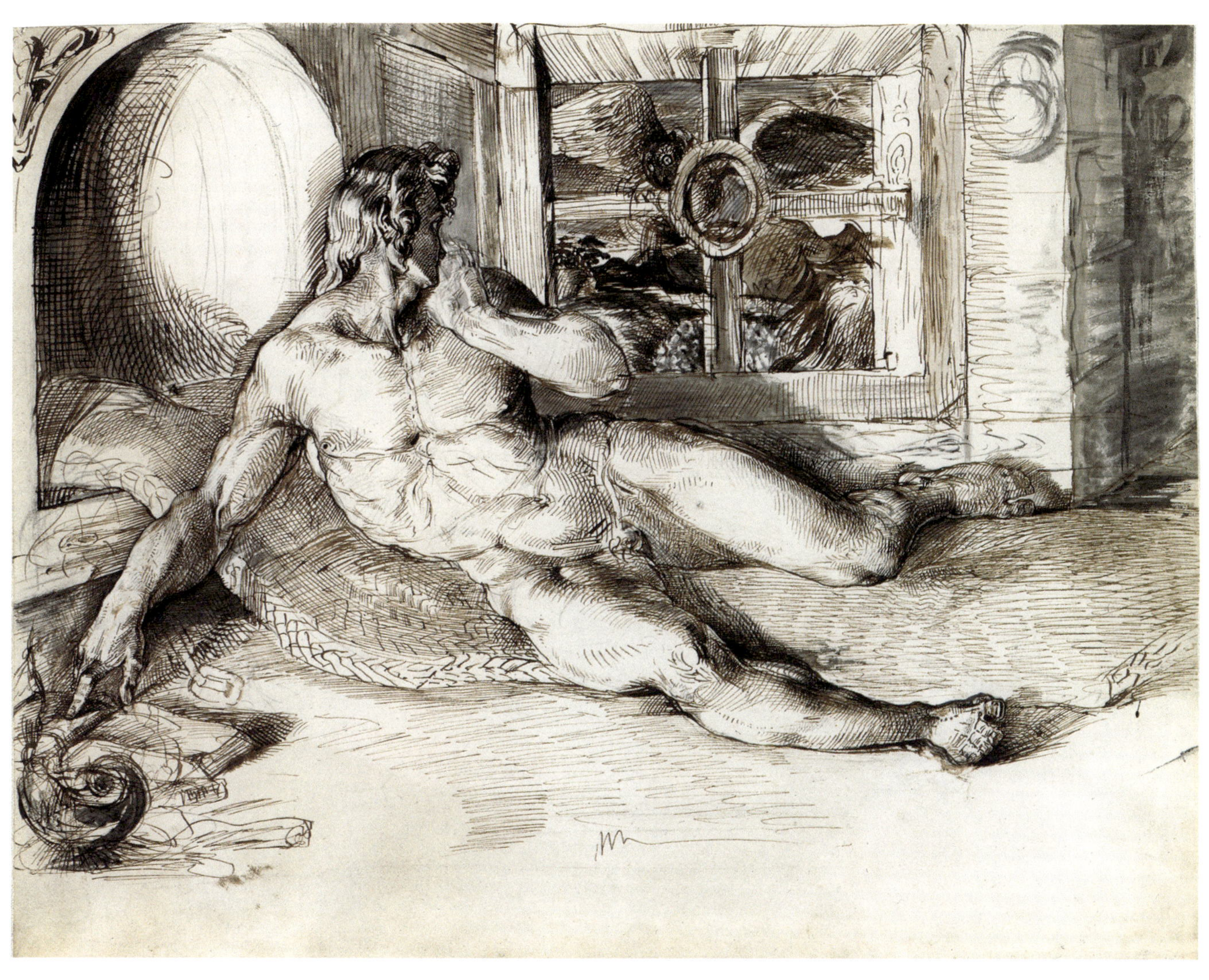

# 30. *Morning—The Early Ploughman,* ca. 1870s

Watercolor and gouache, gum arabic and shell gold, over pencil and traces of charcoal; scratching out; squared in pencil. 9¾ × 7 inches (247 × 178 mm).

Signed at lower left, in point of brush and black ink, *S. PALMER*; inscribed by the artist on verso at upper center in pen and brown ink, *This is 6 sheets thick—Do not let it be thinned by removing paper from the back—S. Palmer*; inscribed at lower right in pencil, *8816*.

PROVENANCE: The Rt. Hon. Sir William Rann Kennedy (1846–1915); by descent; sale, Sotheby's, London, 14 July 1994, lot 157; from which acquired by Artemis Fine Arts Ltd., London; their sale, Christie's, London, 8 June 2000, lot 112, bought in; acquired from Artemis / C. G. Boerner Inc., New York.

BIBLIOGRAPHY: London and New York 2005–6, under no. 140, p. 220.

2001.1

Palmer received his only training from William Wate (d. 1832), with whom he briefly studied drawing. The son of a London book dealer, Palmer grew up with a predilection for the classical poetry of Virgil and that of the seventeenth-century poets Edmund Spenser and John Milton, which would inform his work throughout his long career. In 1822 he met and became a disciple of William Blake (1757–1827), responding to Blake's romantic view of nature as an embodiment of the divine. Under Blake's influence, during the mid-1820s Palmer made drawings in an emphatically primitive style that he never completely abandoned, even as his designs took on attributes of the ideal landscape in the tradition of Claude Lorrain.

The present drawing of a man plowing a field at dawn depicts a subject that occupied Palmer for decades and may have signified for him man's access to the redemptive forces of nature (Cambridge 1984, p. 68). In about 1835–36 he executed a brown wash study, in the British Museum, London, whose vertical composition closely resembles that of the Morgan sheet (Lister 1988, no. 237). The London drawing is squared in pencil and apparently was used by Palmer to prepare his etching *The Early Ploughman,* or *The Morning Spread upon the Mountains,* begun before 1861 (Fig. 1). Horizontal in format, the print features a stand of cypresses in place of the deciduous trees of the brown wash study and adds a bridge over a stream at left. The etching may have been the model for the present drawing, whose pencil squaring lies beneath the media, indicating that the sheet was squared in order to transfer the design from another source. Palmer is known to have made drawings after his prints (Elizabeth Barker, communication with the author, 1 April 2006; see, for example, London and New York 2005–6, nos. 152, 161). The plowman appears in four further drawings, two that are compositionally similar to the etching (Lister 1988, nos. M8, M10; Sotheby's, London, 25 November 2004, lot 204, and Sotheby's, London, 14 July 1988, respectively) and two that are closer in design to the Morgan sheet (Lister 1988, nos. 610, 611; private collection, England, and Sotheby's, London, 15 July 1993, lot 118, respectively).

While a date for the present drawing of about 1863 has been suggested (C. G. Boerner files), the sheet may have been executed much later because of the similarities in technique and handling that it shares with works dated near the end of Palmer's career, such as *The Lonely Tower* (Lister 1988, no. M23; Huntington Library, Art Collections, and Botanical Gardens, San Marino), a poetic watercolor of two figures in a starlit landscape, and *The Bellman* (Lister 1988, no. M19; Trustees of the Cecil Higgins Art Gallery, Bedford), an illustration to Milton's *Il Penseroso*. In all three drawings one finds closely comparable dots and dashes of watercolor and skeins of fine black strokes used to build up forms. KS

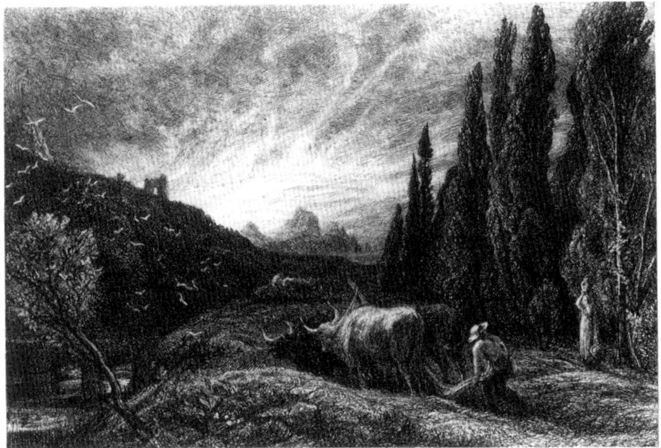

Fig. 1. Samuel Palmer, *The Early Ploughman* (National Gallery of Art, Washington, D.C.)

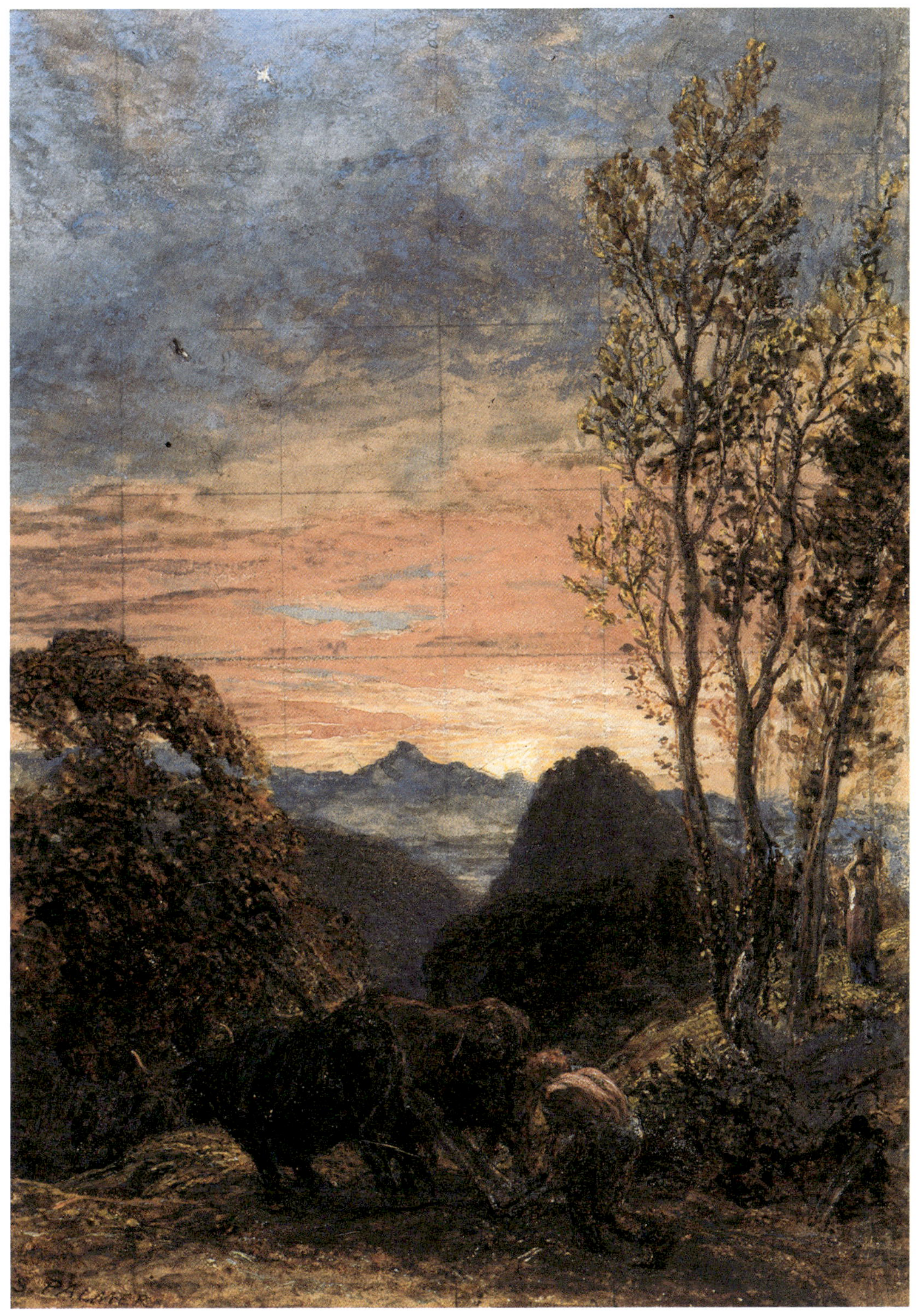

# 31. *Oak Tree near Albano Laziale,* 1772

Pen and black ink and brown and gray wash, over graphite; laid down on old mount. 21 × 14 11/16 inches (536 × 376 mm).

Signed and dated at upper left, in pen and black ink, *à Albano 1772 J. Ph: Hackert f:.* Inscribed on verso of old mount at upper center in pen and blue ink, *HACKERT, Jean Théophile (frère de Philippe, dit Hackert d'Italie Ecole allem. 1744–1773.[ )]*; below this in graphite in the same hand, *ou Philippe, dit Hackert d'Italie. Ecole all. (Prenzlau 1737-–Florence 1807)*; below this in pen and blue ink in the same hand, *daté et signé: "à Albano 1772. J. Th. Hackert f."*; below this in graphite in the same hand, *ou Ph.*; below this in pen and blue ink in the same hand, *"veduté avec pendent de mêmes dimensions et même technique qui porte la mention: 'dans le bois de Rocca di Papa f. 1772'" / Vente publique, salle van Dyck (direct. A. de Tavernier fils Anvers, 27/28 Juin 1921.[ )]*; in graphite in a different hand at upper left, *68/2*, at upper center, *214*; below this, inscribed on a printed label, *441 Hackert (J. Ph.), 1772. Le bois di Papa; Paysage à Albano. 2 / dessins, plume et sépia.*

PROVENANCE: Sale, A. de Tavernier, Fils, Antwerp, 26 June 1921, part of lot 441; acquired from C. G. Boerner Inc., New York.

EXHIBITION: Düsseldorf 1999, no. 8.

2001.3

One of the most celebrated German landscape artists of the eighteenth century and the subject of a biography by Johann Wolfgang von Goethe (1749–1832), Jacob Philipp Hackert studied with his father, Philipp Hackert, a portraitist and animal painter, before enrolling in the Royal Academy of Art in Berlin, where he copied the landscapes of Claude Lorrain (1600–1682) and those of the Dutch masters. After sojourns in Sweden and France, he settled permanently in Italy in 1768, enjoying the patronage of Catherine II and Paul I of Russia, Pope Pius VI, and King Ferdinand IV of Naples, becoming Ferdinand's court painter. An early advocate of working en plein air, he produced drawings and paintings that were esteemed for their accurate and sensitive response to nature while conforming to the conventions of the ideal, classical landscape in the manner of Claude Lorrain.

The present drawing embodies both these traditions. It represents a view along a wooded path in the Alban Hills, about twenty miles southeast of Rome. This picturesque region was a popular tourist destination in the late eighteenth century and famous for its oak and chestnut trees. Hackert's subject was the monumental oak tree that almost fills the composition. Heeding his own advice, he depicted the tree with such care that it is identifiable to the botanist (Marie Long, correspondence with the author, 21 July 2006; Hackert, p. 234, cited in Mitchell 1989, p. 650). Following the conventions of the ideal landscape, modified to accommodate the vertical composition, Hackert depicted a view unfolding to distant hills beyond the tree stump at left and placed a group of diminutive figures at right to emphasize the enormous scale of the tree. The buildings along the far horizon may be those of Castel Gandolfo, one of the hill towns of the region and site of the summer papal residence.

As was his practice, Hackert likely began the drawing on site by sketching the outlines of the composition, adding in the studio delicate gray and brown washes in a range of closely gradated tones that give the work its richness and high degree of finish. Signed and dated, the drawing probably was intended for the market among northern European travelers on the Grand Tour.

Trees in all their formal variety became a dominant feature in Hackert's oeuvre with his arrival in Italy and remained so throughout his career. From 1769 onward, he made not only tree studies but also fully developed, often vertical, compositions, in both paintings and drawings, with a single monumental tree dominating the design (see, for example, Nordhoff 1994, pls. 27, 152, 274, 302, and 304). A late example is *In the Valley of Diana*, a drawing signed by the artist and dated 1796 (Kupferstichkabinett, Berlin; Nordhoff 1994, no. 892, pl. 606). As he observed in his treatise "On Landscape Art," thought to have been written in the 1790s, "nothing is as pleasing, in nature as well as in a drawing or painting, as a beautiful tree" (Hackert, p. 235, cited in Mitchell 1989, p. 650).

KS

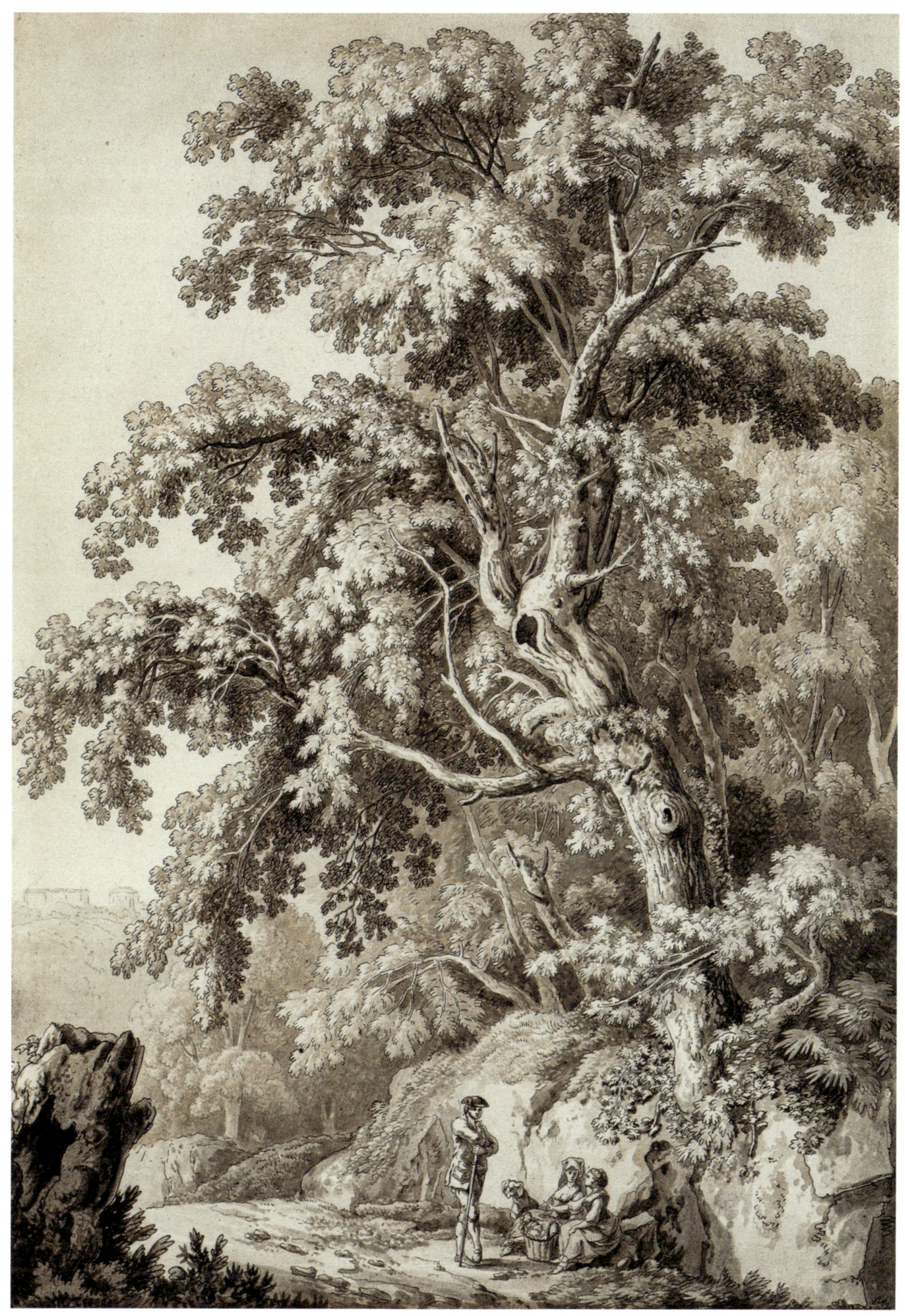

# 32. *Landscape near Kiel in Schleswig-Holstein,* 1814

Black chalk on wove paper; ruled border in black chalk. 5⅞ × 9½ inches (150 × 242 mm).

Inscribed by the artist and dated in pencil, at lower left, *Kiel den 27. August 1814.*

PROVENANCE: The artist's family; sale, C. G. Boerner, Leipzig, 28 April 1939, no. 19, pl. III; private collection, Germany; acquired from C. G. Boerner, Inc., New York.

EXHIBITIONS: Düsseldorf and New York 1992, no. 65; New York 1996, no. 31; New York 1997.

1996.7

The German romantic artist Friedrich Olivier trained with his elder brother Ferdinand (1785–1841). In 1811 the two settled in Vienna, where they joined the circle of artists connected to the Guild of St. Luke, later known as the Nazarenes, founded in 1809 by Franz Pforr (1788–1812) and Friedrich Overbeck (1789–1869) in opposition to the strictures of academic training and committed to reviving the art of the German Middle Ages and early Renaissance.

Following military service in 1813–14 in Germany and Belgium during the Wars of Liberation against Napoleon's armies, the younger Olivier returned to Vienna, remaining until 1817. The drawings he made during these years, such as *The Pilgrim* of 1817 (Kupferstichkabinett, Dresden; New York 1988–89, no. 71), were inspired by the precise draftsmanship and religious and allegorical subject matter of the Nazarene artists Julius Schnorr von Carolsfeld (1794–1872) and Joseph Anton Koch (1768–1839), with whom he associated in Vienna.

In 1818 the Olivier brothers traveled with Schnorr von Carolsfeld to Rome. Friedrich returned to Vienna in 1823 and in 1829 settled in Munich, where he collaborated with Schnorr von Carolsfeld on the Nibelungenlied frescos in the Residenz. In 1850 he returned to Dessau.

The present drawing is one of the earliest known by the artist. Executed during his military service, it represents a landscape in the city of Kiel, on the Baltic Sea in northern Germany. Using a piece of black chalk sharpened to a fine point, he recorded the view of a quiet farmscape with delicacy and great immediacy, conveying the hot stillness of a late summer day. The design consists mostly of meadow and sky, with a farmhouse at right tucked behind a screen of trees and another building at left seeming almost to grow out of the foliage. The diagonal line of the meadow leads the eye to the farmhouse in the background at right and then to the top of the tree, towering incongruously above the others and silhouetted against an expanse of sky. Olivier included an isolated pair of unusually tall trees in *The Burial,* an allegorical subject dated 1815 (Akademie, Vienna; Grote 1999, fig. 84).

In contrast to the sharp linearity characteristic of drawings by his fellow Nazarene Schnorr von Carolsfeld, Olivier's drawings often display a softness of line reminiscent of that produced by a burin in making an etching. The row of trees screening the farmhouse at right in the present drawing echoes the distinctive cauliflower-like trees found in the oeuvre of the early-seventeenth-century Dutch printmaker Hercules Seghers.

KS

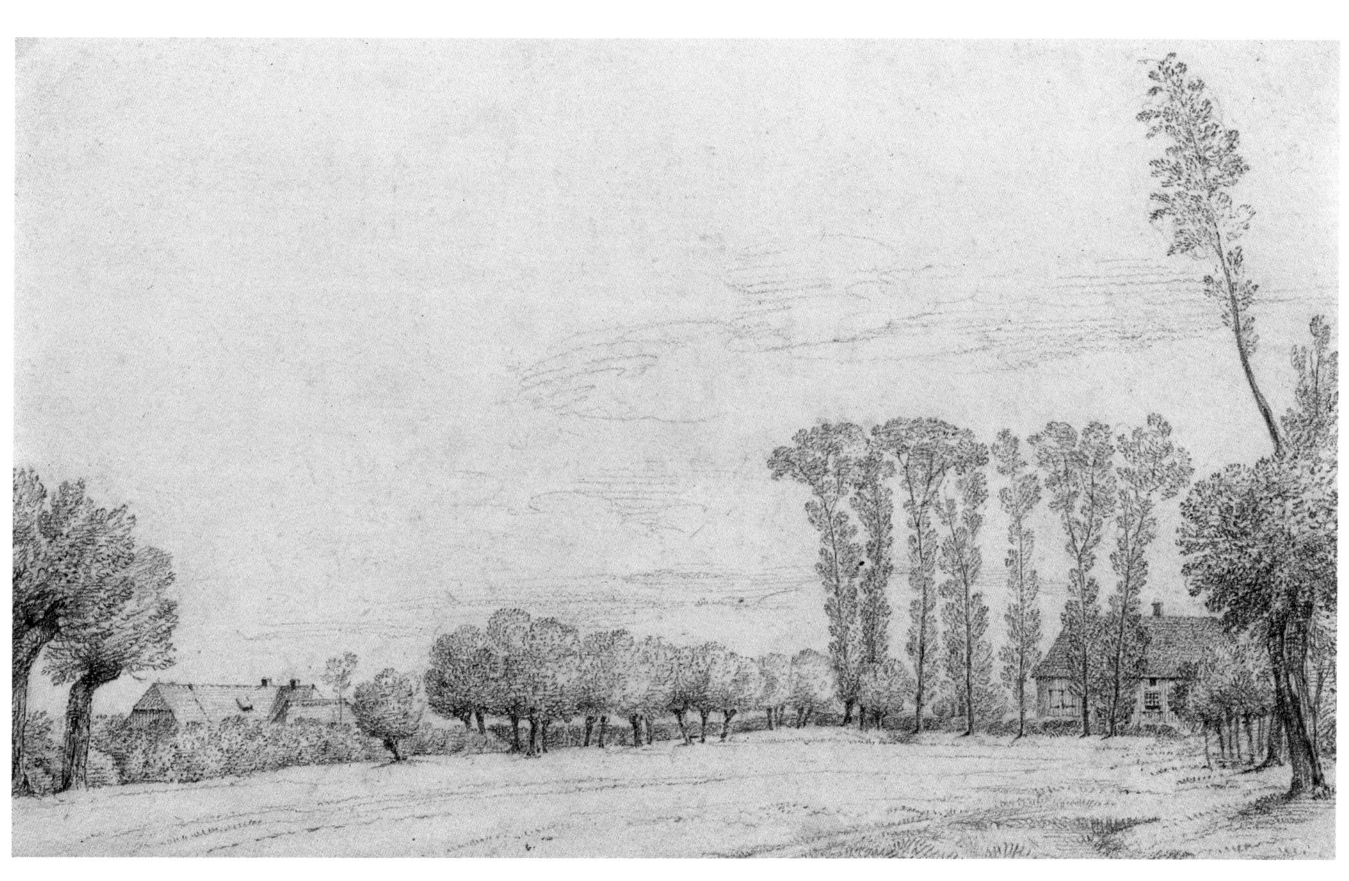

EUGÈNE DELACROIX French, Charenton-Saint-Maurice 1798–1863 Paris

# 33. *Seated Arab,* ca. 1832

Watercolor over graphite, with point of brush and black ink. 11⅞ × 8⅛ inches (302 × 208 mm).

Atelier stamp in red ink at lower right, *ED.*

PROVENANCE: Delacroix atelier sale (Lugt S. 838a); Hervé Robichon de la Guérinière, Château du Roc, Creyesse, Dordogne; Galerie Claude Aubry, Paris; Walter Feilchenfeldt, Zurich; private collection, New York (since 1977); acquired from Walter Feilchenfeldt, Zurich.

1997.1

The significance of traveling through North Africa to Delacroix's career has been well documented. In 1832 he first ventured as part of a diplomatic delegation dispatched by Louis-Philippe and led by the elegant and cultivated Count Charles de Mornay to Moulay Abd al-Rahman in French-occupied Algeria. This trip led him briefly through Spain and throughout Morocco and Algeria for nearly five months.

An inveterate draftsman, Delacroix recorded the people in North Africa and their surroundings in numerous sketchbooks and drawings during his stay. He was fascinated by his direct experience of an exotic environment. Upon arriving in Tangiers on 25 January 1832, in a letter to his friend Jean-Baptiste Pierret he enthusiastically explained, "One would need to have twenty arms and forty-eight hours a day to give any tolerable impression of it all . . . at the moment I'm like a man in a dream, seeing things he's afraid will vanish from him" (Delacroix 2001, p. 181). This need to capture everything inspired the artist to draw continually during his stay. He later employed many of these sketches as aide-mémoire for paintings and watercolors following his return to France.

This sheet comprises a principal study drawn in graphite and tinted with wash, of an Arab chieftain wearing a white burnoose and an ocher cloak, and ancillary graphite studies of the folds of his turban, his standing figure, and his upturned face. Delacroix recorded his particular reaction to the dignified bearing and costume of the chieftains in an oft-quoted letter to Pierret, "All of them in white, like Roman senators or Greeks at the Panathenean festival" (Delacroix 2001, pp. 187–88). He also recounted his strategy to produce such frank depictions of his sitters as in the present sheet: "I am gradually insinuating myself into the customs of the country, so as to be able to draw many of these Moorish figures quite freely. They have very strong prejudices against the noble art of painting, but a few coins slipped here and there settle their scruples" (Delacroix to Pierret and Félix Guillemardet, 8 February 1832; Delacroix 2001, pp. 182–84). Here the artist portrayed his sitter swiftly and directly. Unlike some of Delacroix's more casual notations, this study is a more formal and purposeful rendering of a particular sitter, perhaps the same one depicted in profile on another sheet (see Paris 1994–95, no. 22, repr., private collection). The almost ethnographic interest in his Arab sitters raises these watercolors above simple costume and figure studies, nearer to enigmatic portraits. JT

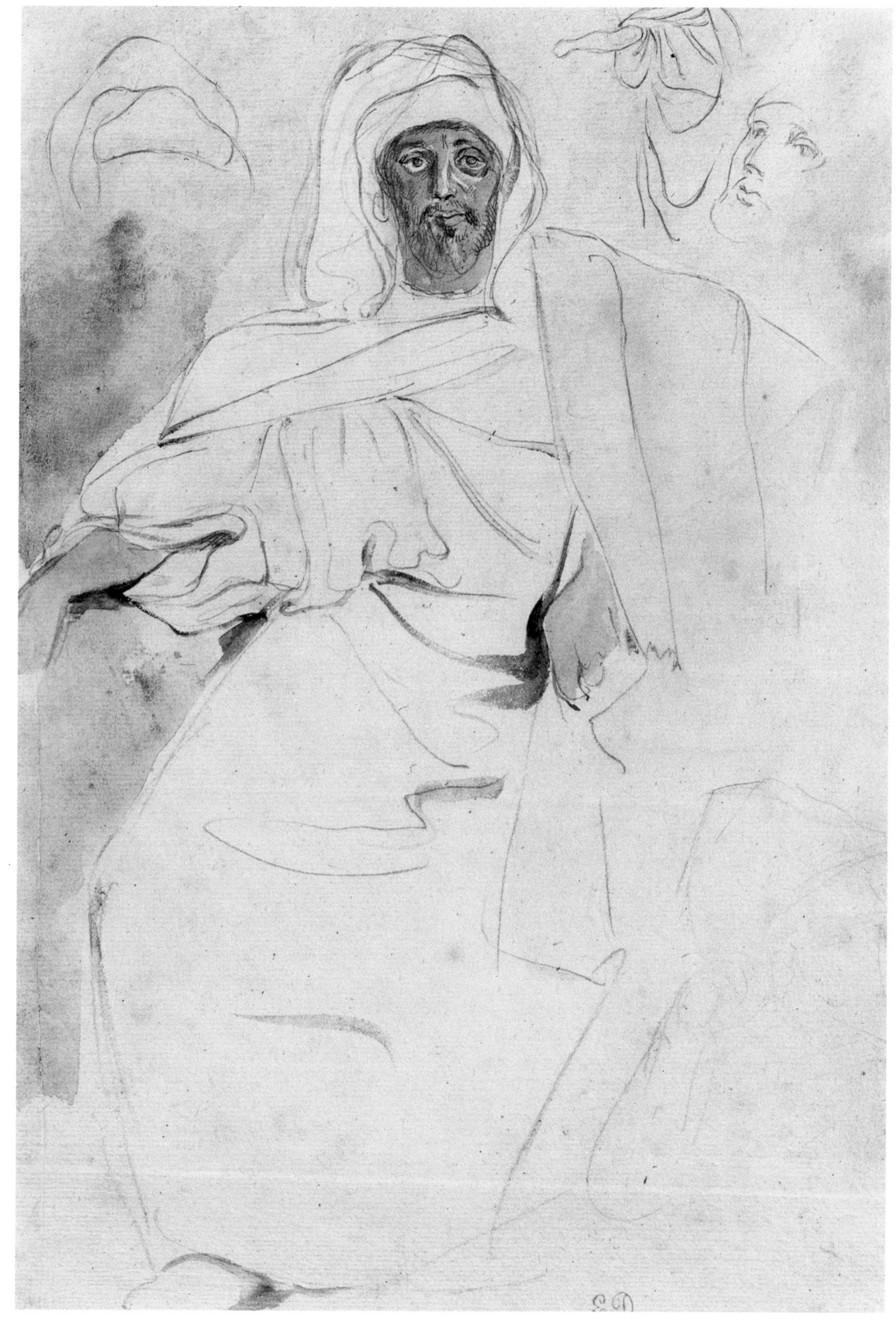

EDWARD LEAR British, Holloway, London, 1812–1888 San Remo, Italy

# 34. *The Grand Canal with Santa Maria della Salute, Venice,* 1865

Watercolor, some gouache, over graphite. 13 13/16 × 19 7/8 inches (351 × 503 mm).

Inscribed by the artist at lower left in pen and brown ink, *Venice. 3PM. 13 Nov<sup>r</sup>. 1865 / (from the steps of the Iron bridge.) white papers on windows of lodgings.*; numbered at lower right, / 20 /, and further inscribed with the artist's color notes, including twice at left center in pencil and in pen and brown ink, *gorgeous bright ocher,* at center in pen and brown ink, *calm blue.*

PROVENANCE: Private collection, until 1997; sale, Christie's, London, 8 April 1997, lot 108; private collection; sale, Cheffins, Cambridge, 28 April 2005, lot 600, bought in; acquired from Andrew Clayton-Payne Ltd., London.

BIBLIOGRAPHY: London 1985, under no. 59.

2006.1

Best known for his limericks, published as *A Book of Nonsense* (1846), and the children's poem *The Owl and the Pussycat* (1871), Lear was almost entirely self-taught as an artist. His earliest work was as an ornithological draftsman, and in 1830–32 he published *Illustrations of the Family of Psittacidae, or Parrots,* a set of lithographed plates after his drawings. By 1834, he had begun making landscape drawings employing the precise draftsmanship he practiced as a natural history illustrator (New Haven 2000, p. 14). In 1837 he visited Rome and, except for brief interludes, lived the rest of his life abroad, traveling throughout the Mediterranean, the Near East, Africa, and South Asia and producing thousands of drawings of the sites he visited.

The present drawing is a study for a painting of 1866 commissioned by Frances, Countess Waldegrave (private collection; London 1985, no. 59). Executed during a sojourn in Venice in November 1865, the drawing represents a view from the Iron Bridge down the Grand Canal to the church of Santa Maria della Salute. As we know from Lear's inscription, he executed the drawing on 13 November at three o'clock in the afternoon. At eight o'clock that morning he recorded a view of Santa Maria della Salute from the Doge's Palace (private collection; London 1985, no. 31). Lear subsequently made a painting of the second design that was bought by Henry Willett in 1873 (art market; London 1981, no. 18, cited in London 1985, p. 152).

In Lear's diary for 13 November 1865 he referred to both drawings: "Had a cup of cafe noir in the Hotel—& then got a gondola for the day. First drew S[anta] M[aria] de[lla] S[alute] by the Doge's Palace—then from the Iron Bridge . . . but it was very cold." Three days later he wrote, "The same bright gorgeous—but cold weather. Anything so indescribably beautiful as the colour of the place I never saw" (cited in London 1985, p. 116).

In the present drawing, Lear captured the crystal clarity of a bright, cold late-autumn day. Although his color notes on the sheet describe the water as "calm blue," the parallel- and cross-hatching in the lower left quadrant create a staccato rhythm that may correspond to the chill he felt sketching in the open air. Lear, who visited Venice only twice—the first time in 1857—rarely depicted cityscapes, preferring open landscape and the elements of nature (London 1985, p. 152). This predilection may account for his concentration on water and sky in this drawing. An anonymous photograph of about 1885 recording the precise view drawn by Lear (Stainton 1985, frontispiece) reveals how faithfully he represented his subject.

KS

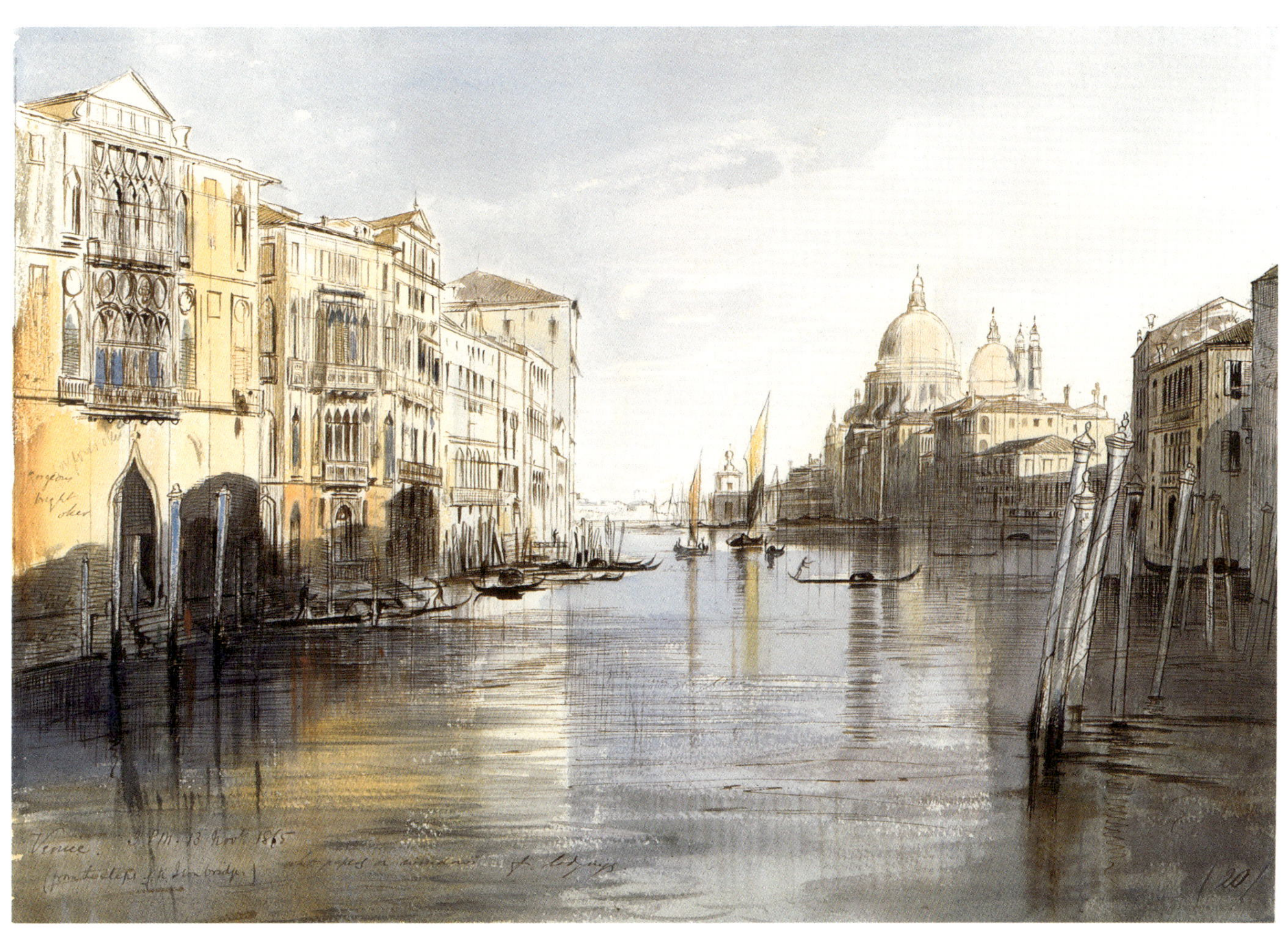

# 35. *Figure of a Man Unbinding His Sash,* ca. 1851

Black chalk, stumped, heightened with white chalk, on brown wove paper. 11½ × 8⅝ inches (292 × 219 mm).

Inscribed at upper right in pencil, *X*; inscribed on verso at upper center, *Kat. 176*, and at lower center, *Lila Wappe[n]*.

PROVENANCE: Unidentified collector (coat of arms on recto); presumably acquired from the artist by Hermann Pächter (d. 1906), Berlin (owner of Kunsthandlung R. Wagner, Berlin); from whom acquired by Königliche National-Galerie, Berlin, 1889; to Leo Lewin, Breslau (in exchange for drawings by Max Slevogt), 1927–28; [his?] sale, Rudolph Lepke's Kunstauctions-Haus, Berlin, 23 February 1932, lot 175; [possibly Linz Museum, 1942]; K. H. Schönfeld (not in Lugt); sale, Karl & Faber, Munich, 7 December 1989, lot 495; from which acquired by C. G. Boerner, Düsseldorf (later Artemis Fine Arts Inc., New York); from whom acquired.

BIBLIOGRAPHY: Donop 1902, no. 176; Berlin 1905, no. 526 (not repr.).

EXHIBITIONS: Düsseldorf 1990, no. 27; Leipzig 1990–91, no. 107; New York 1997.

1996.155

The greatest German draftsman of the nineteenth century, Menzel was largely self-taught. He trained with his father, a former school headmaster who founded a lithographic press, which Adolph took over at age sixteen, when his father died. His earliest works were as a printmaker, and his distinctive graphic manner—fine strokes alternating with dramatic, broader accents, occasionally softened by smudging—developed from his handling of chalk in the preparation of lithographs.

This technique is evident in the present drawing, a study for the wood engraving of 1851 depicting the Prussian general Hans Karl von Winterfeldt (1707–1757; Fig. 1). Menzel made the print as one of a series of twelve three-quarter-length woodcut portraits of Frederick the Great (1712–1786) and his generals, commissioned in 1850 and published in Berlin in 1856, *The Time of King Frederick: Heroes of War and Peace* (Bock 1991, nos. 1065–76). An avid student of history and passionate admirer of the German leader, Menzel first worked on a project connected with Frederick in 1839 when he was commissioned to produce about four hundred wood engravings illustrating *The History of Frederick the Great* (Leipzig, 1840–42).

Drawn with vigor and supreme confidence in his favored medium at the time, this sheet is one of three known studies of the subject. Another is in the Kupferstichkabinett, Staatliche Museen zu Berlin (Donop 1902, no. 175; Cambridge 1984, no. 39); the whereabouts of the third are unknown (Donop 1902, no. 177). The Morgan drawing is more finished than the sheet in Berlin, despite the cropping of the design along the upper margin, a feature it shares with the Berlin drawing. The pose of the figure in the Morgan drawing is also closer to the print than it is in the Berlin sheet and may have been one of the last studies Menzel executed before transferring the design to the woodblock. He likely drew the figure from a model, as he did in the 1852 chalk drawing *Study of Model for Frederick II in an Armchair* in the Kupferstichkabinett, Berlin (Paris and elsewhere 1996–97, no. 62). The features of the head and face in the print probably were copied after a contemporary portrait of von Winterfeldt and documented in drawings by Menzel not yet identified.

Menzel depicted his subject in the three-quarter-length format commonly used for seventeenth-century engraved portraits of aristocrats, but its relaxed sensibility—also seen in other portraits in the series—sets it apart from these earlier works. As Susanne von Falkenhausen observed, Menzel, possessed of a "non-aristocratic eye," chose to portray the Prussian general in an intimate moment after removing his tricorn hat and while unbinding his sash (Cambridge 1984, p. 76). A defining characteristic of Menzel's contemporary portraits, this humanness is found in his likenesses of historical figures as well, bringing long-dead personages fully to life (see, for example, his portrait of Shakespeare; Bock 1991, no. 1064). KS

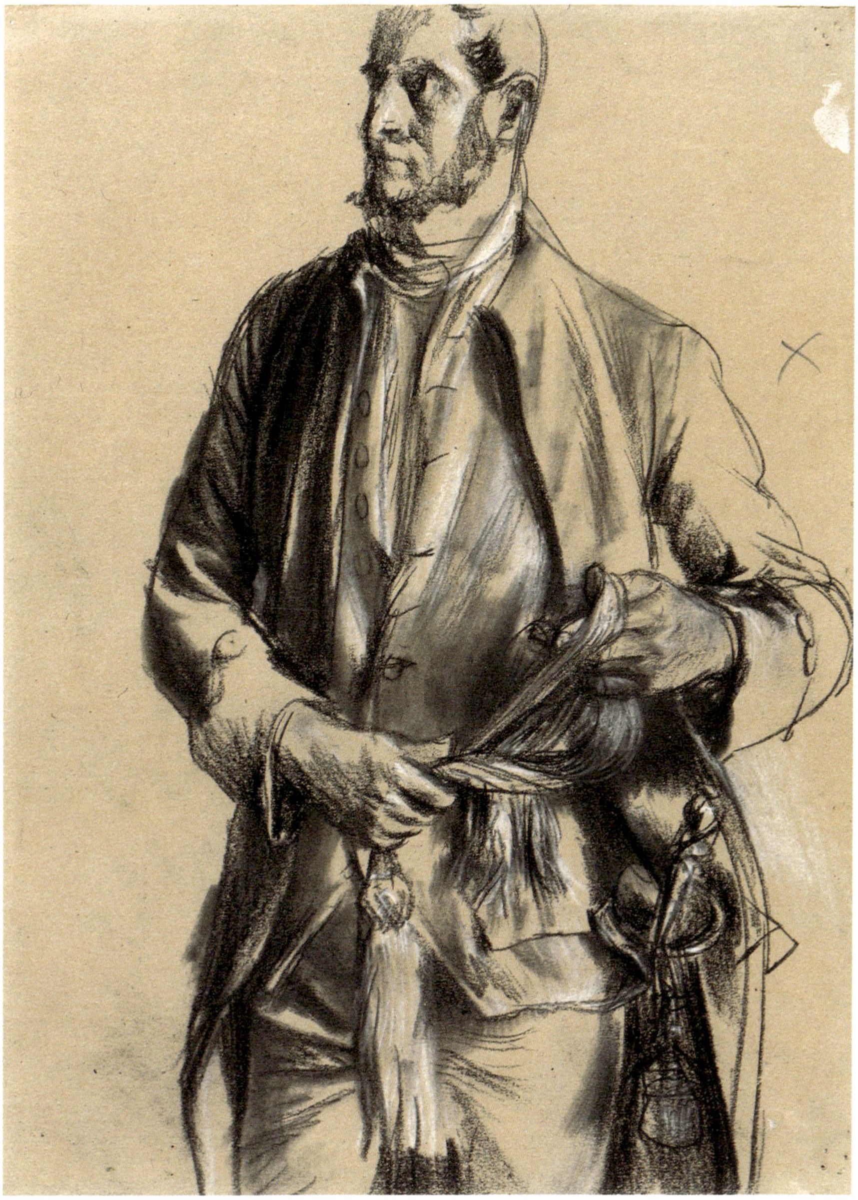

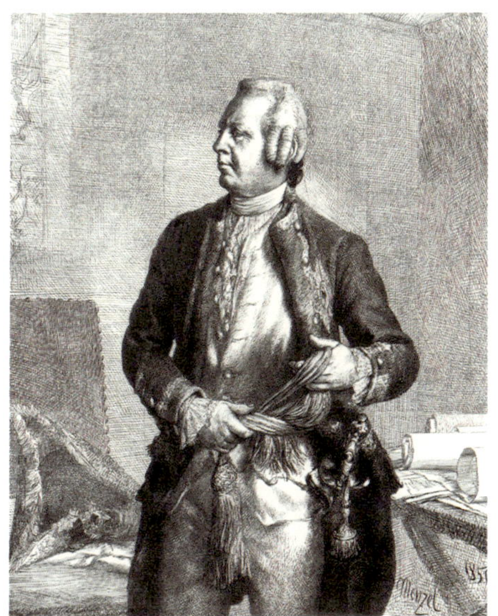

Fig. 1. *Hans Karl von Winterfeldt,* in *The Time of King Frederick: Heroes of War and Peace,* Berlin, 1856 (New York Public Library)

HENRI-JOSEPH HARPIGNIES French, Valenciennes 1819–1916 Saint-Privé, Yonne

# 36. *View of the Basilica of Maxentius (Later Basilica of Constantine) in the Roman Forum,* 1869

Watercolor over graphite on wove paper. 19⅛ × 29¼ inches (484 × 742 mm).

Signed and dated in brush and black ink, at lower left, *Hj Harpignies. 1869.*

PROVENANCE: The Reid Gallery, London; Arthur Tooth Gallery, London; The Honorable Sir John Millar, Monaco; acquired from Galerie Hopkins-Thomas, Paris.

EXHIBITIONS: London 1960, no. 8, repr.; New York 2002, no. 73.

1996.1

Although he is often classified as an artist of the Barbizon school, Harpignies did not retreat to the town and its forest to work. He did, however, take up the landscape as his principal subject. He was influenced substantially by the work of Jean-Baptiste-Camille Corot (1796–1875), whose rendering of nature and light effects, especially in his Italian subjects, shaped Harpignies's aesthetic. He worked alongside the Dutch painter Johan Barthold Jongkind (1819–1891), an elder cohort of the impressionists, who frequently employed watercolor on a large scale. Harpignies's first trip to Rome was at the outset of his career, in 1850–51; it was then that he began to use watercolor. Returning to France, he initially exhibited at the Salon in 1853 and would continue to do so regularly until 1912.

Harpignies left Paris for Italy a second time after his submissions to the annual Salon in 1863 were rejected. There his style matured, and he returned to exhibit at the Salon again, earning medals in 1866, 1868, and 1869. He was awarded the silver medal in 1878 for his view of the Colosseum (Musée d'Orsay, Paris), reflecting the continued importance of Italian subjects to his work. Jules-Antoine Castagnary charted Harpignies's progress at the Salon, and in 1868 rejoiced that "Harpignies is not only the excellent landscapist that you know, he is also one of the most renowned among our watercolorists" (Castagnary 1892, vol. 1, p. 319). The artist executed this large watercolor in 1869, long after his return to Paris, at the height of his newfound success, and a year before he would enter military service during the Franco-Prussian War. It must have been based on an earlier sketch done in Rome and suggests the lasting impact of the experience on Harpignies's career. In fact, he faithfully reprised the composition in another watercolor nearly a decade later (Amsterdam 1972, no. 64, repr.).

The panoramic view of the ruins and surrounding city unfolds over the broad horizontal of the sheet. It is taken from the grassy rise of the Palatine Hill, emerging from the woods on a path terminating in rocks and brush. At the edge of nature there is a vista of the ruined fourth-century Basilica of Maxentius (also known as the Basilica of Constantine) embraced by the encroaching houses and dazzling in the brilliant sunlight. The basilica was begun by Maxentius in A.D. 308 and completed by Constantine after he defeated Maxentius at the Battle of the Milvian Bridge in A.D. 312. The ruins of the Roman Forum, including the basilica, with its massive arcades, were a favorite subject of artists in Rome from Giovanni Battista Piranesi to Corot. Harpignies's famed views of the Colosseum also depict the ruins from the wooded fringe of the city.

JT

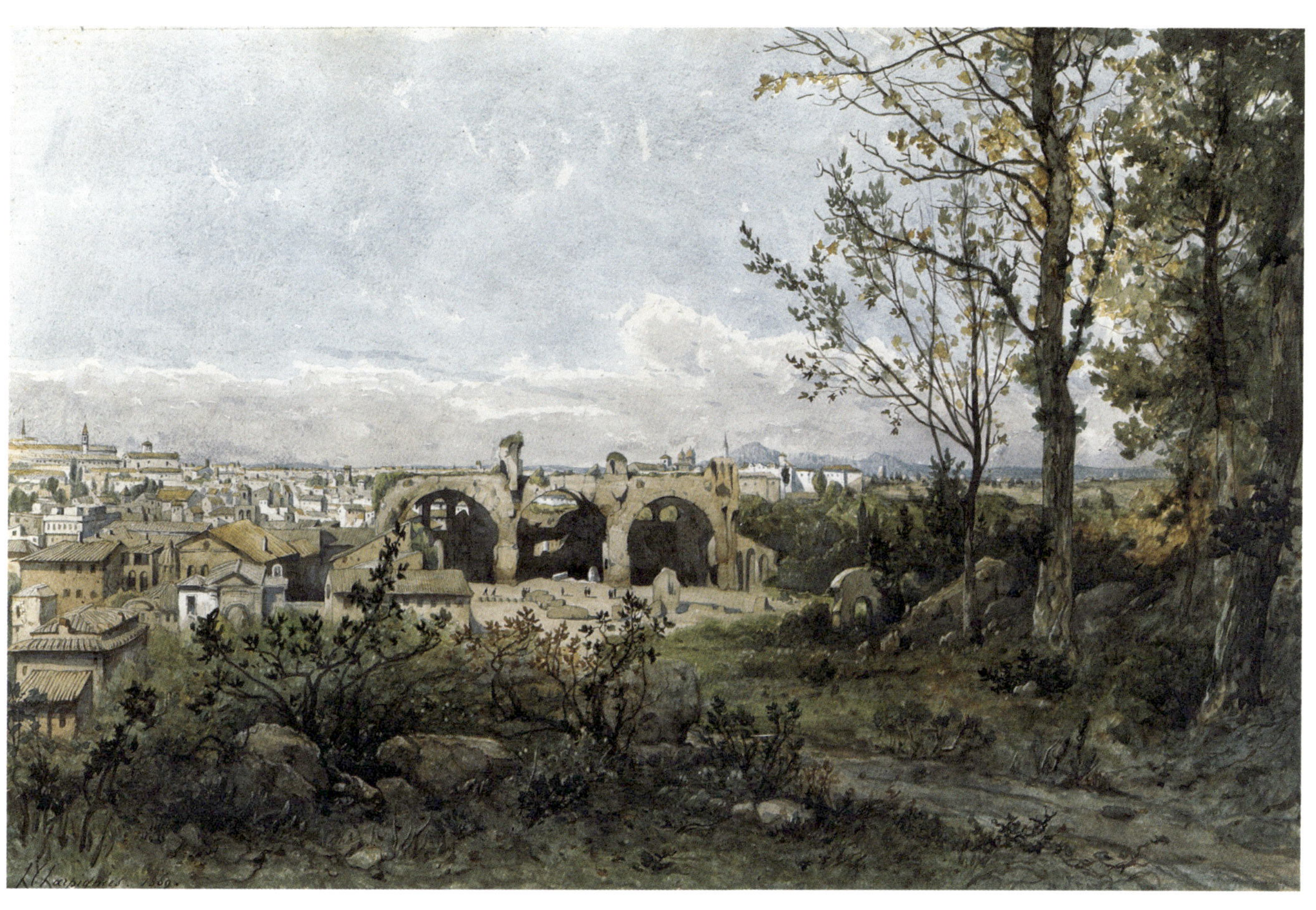

REX WHISTLER British, London 1905–1944 Normandy

# 37. *The Mermaid: Design for a Cave Room Mural*, 1929

Watercolor, heightened with white gouache, over traces of black chalk; ruled in pencil; lined. Sheet: 9¾ × 11 1/16 inches (247 × 281 mm). Design: 6¼ × 8⅞ inches (158 × 224 mm).

Signed and dated below bottom edge of design at right in pen and black ink, *Rex Whistler. 1929.*; inscribed by the artist below design in pen and brown ink, *Edge of door to be moulded in plaster. / Everything else painted. / Floor of room. / Design for a 'Cave' room;* on verso, according to previous literature, but not visible because of lining, *For Mary with love and best wishes from Rex. 19 July 1935.*

WATERMARK: Fragment (half moon and star, Egypten; countermark of three stars and half moon).

PROVENANCE: Presented by the artist to Lady Mary Dunn (Lady Mary Campbell), 1935 (the date according to Whistler 1960); Derrick Morley (by 1960, the date according to Whistler 1960); sale, Phillip's, Bath (U.K.), 27 March 2000; from which acquired by Thomas Agnew & Sons Ltd., London; Thomas Deans Fine Art, Inc., Atlanta, 2003; Thomas Agnew & Sons Ltd., London, 2005; acquired from W/S Fine Art Ltd., London.

BIBLIOGRAPHY: Whistler 1960, no. 262, p. 40, pl. 60.

EXHIBITIONS: London 1960, no. 62, p. 19; London 2002, no. 96.

2006.6

Whistler studied in London at the Royal Academy of Arts Schools and the Slade School of Fine Art, where he was considered one of the most promising artists of his generation. He built a successful career as a muralist and book illustrator, executing wall paintings in private houses—the most important for Lord Anglesey at Plas Newydd, Isle of Anglesey, Wales, in 1936–38 (Whistler 1960, no. 12, pls. 20–24)—and creating hand-colored pen drawings for such projects as Jonathan Swift's *Gulliver's Travels* (London, 1931). His most famous project is the mural for the restaurant at the Tate Gallery, London, *The Expedition in Pursuit of Rare Meats*, completed in 1927, when he was twenty-three years old (Willsdon 2000, pp. 368–70, 372, pls. 215, 216). Whistler also executed portraits of members of London society, including Dame Edith Sitwell of about 1929 (private collection; Whistler 1960, no. 103, not repr.) and Cecil Beaton of about 1935 (private collection; Whistler 1960, no. 123, not repr.). He died on his first day of action on the coast of Normandy during service in World War II.

This drawing is a study for a projected design, apparently never realized, for a mural representing an underwater cave or grotto. In this highly romantic image, executed in the artist's characteristic delicate watercolor washes applied in a miniaturist technique, a mermaid reclines on a rocky shore at the grotto's edge, while behind her lies a ruined ship at anchor with a medieval castle on the far shore. Whistler executed this study the year following a visit to Italy, where he was enthralled with the grottoes of Neptune and the Sirens at Tivoli (Whistler 1985, p. 143). In the same year he also painted an overmantel representing the sea gods Glaucus and Scylla for Robert Carrier's house in Memphis, Tennessee.

Whistler employed similar figures in two of his most important projects undertaken around the time he made the present drawing. A mermaid figure comparable to that seen here appears in his design for a plate in *Gulliver's Travels* by Jonathan Swift (Whistler 1948, p. 52). Another appears in the tailpiece for Part II of *Gulliver's Travels* (Whistler 1948, p. 55). A sunken ship close to that in the present drawing is represented in the title-page design for *Desert Islands* by Walter de la Mare (Faber, 1930; Whistler 1960, no. 427, not repr.; Whistler 1948, p. 60).

The Morgan preserves two other drawings by Whistler, *The Satyr and the Traveler* and *The Two Springs* (PML 127692.2–3), which he executed about 1930 for a proposed illustrated volume of Aesop's Fables, like the present drawing, also never realized. KS

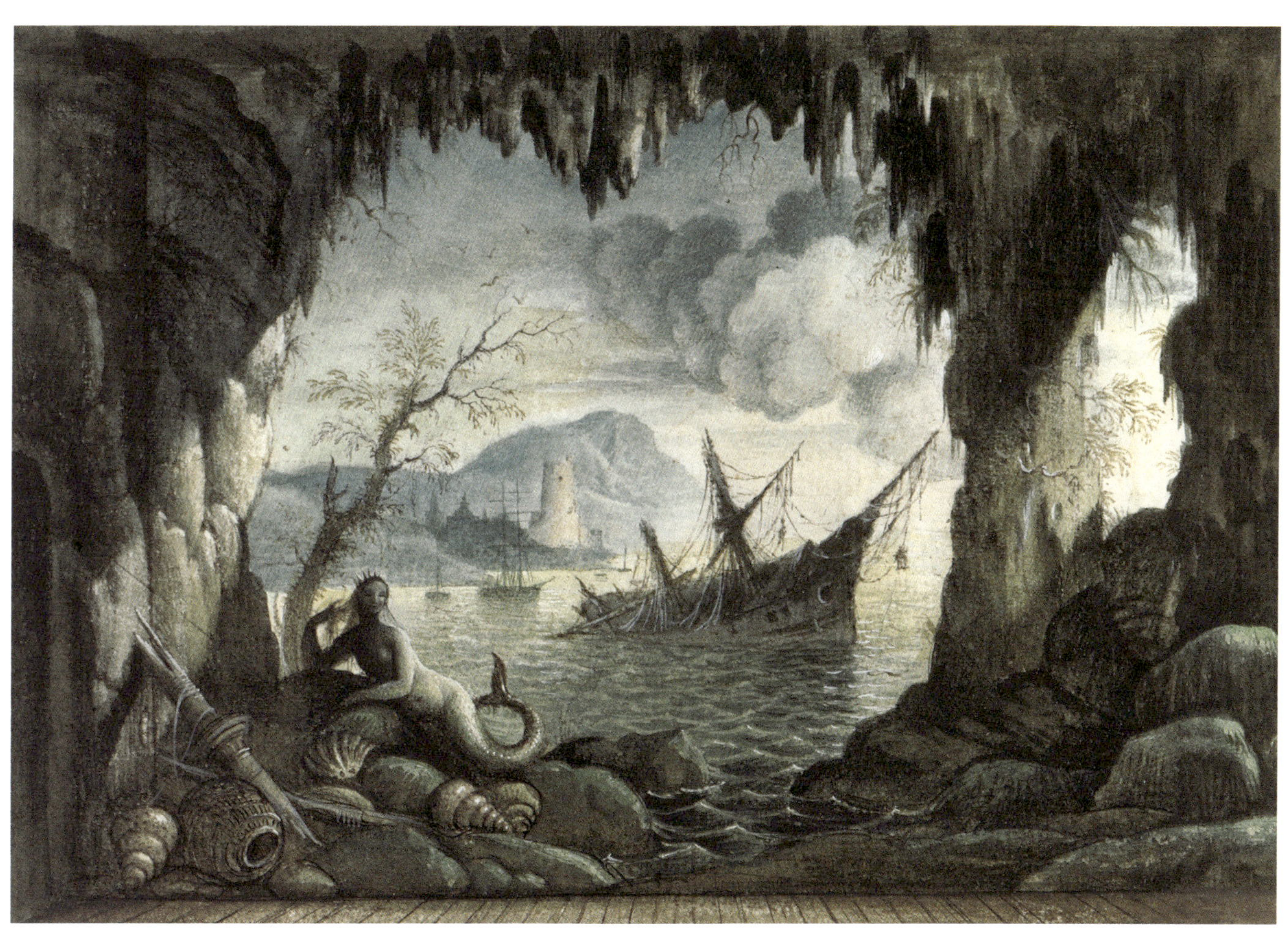

# *Works Cited in Abbreviated Form*

BIBLIOGRAPHY


**Adams 1973**
Eric Adams, *Francis Danby: Varieties of Poetic Landscape*, New Haven and London, 1973.

**Alexander (forthcoming)**
David Alexander, *Dictionary of British Engravers 1714–1830*, forthcoming.

**Almeida and Gilpin 2005**
Hermione de Almeida and George H. Gilpin, *Indian Renaissance: British Romantic Art and the Prospect of India*, Aldershot, England, 2005.

**Archer 1980**
Mildred Archer, *Early Views of India: The Picturesque Journeys of Thomas and William Daniell, 1786–1794*, London, 1980.

**Archer 1996**
Mildred Archer, "Daniell," in *The Dictionary of Art*, vol. 8, New York, 1996, p. 505.

**Arisi 1986**
Ferdinando Arisi, *Gian Paolo Panini e i fasti della Roma del '700*, Rome, 1986.

***Artemis* 1998**
*Artemis 96–97*, New York, 1998.

***Artemis* 2000**
*Artemis 98–99: Consolidated Audited Annual Report*, Luxembourg, 2000.

**Baetjer 1995**
Katherine Baetjer, *European Paintings in the Metropolitan Museum of Art by Artists Born Before 1865*, New York, 1995.

**Ballantine 1866**
J. Ballantine, *The Life of David Roberts, R.A., Compiled from His Journals and Other Sources*, Edinburgh, 1866.

**Bell and Girtin 1935**
C. F. Bell and T. Girtin, "The Drawings and Sketches of John Robert Cozens," *The Walpole Society*, vol. 23, 1935.

**Benjamin 1910**
Lewis Saul Benjamin, *The Life and Letters of William Beckford of Fonthill . . . By Lewis Melville* [pseud.], London, 1910.

**Bocher 1882**
E. Bocher, *J. M. Moreau le Jeune*, Paris, 1882.

**Bock 1991**
Elfried Bock, *Adolph Menzel: Verzeichnis seines graphischen Werkes*, 2nd edition, San Francisco, 1991.

**Boppe 1911**
Auguste Boppe, *Les peintres du Bosphore au dix-huitième siècle*, Paris, 1911.

**Borne 1998**
François Borne, "Diplomatic Encounters," *Christie's Magazine*, July–Aug. 1998, p. 42.

**Boyé 1936**
Pierre Boyé, "Le Chancelier Chaumont de La Galaizière et sa famille," Part II, *Le Pays Lorrain* 28, no. 12 (December 1936), pp. 537–52.

**Brocklebank 1911**
Thomas Brocklebank, *A Catalogue of Paintings, Drawings, Engravings and Etchings in the Possession of T. Brocklebank, at Wateringbury Place, Kent*, London, 1911.

**Castagnary 1892**
Jules Castagnary, *Salons (1857–1870)*, Paris, 1892.

**Chiarini and Padovani 2003**
Marco Chiarini and Serena Padovani, *La Galleria Palatina e gli Appartamenti Reali di Palazzo Pitti. Catalogo dei Dipinti*, vol. 2, Florence, 2003.

**Clayton-Payne 2007**
Andrew Clayton-Payne, *[Selected Works]*, London, 2007.

**Constable 1953**
W. G. Constable, *Richard Wilson*, London, 1953.

**Cook and Wedderburn 1903–12**
E. T. Cook and Alexander Wedderburn, eds., *The Works of John Ruskin*, 39 vols., London and New York, 1903–12.

**Cuzin 1987**
J.-P. Cuzin, *François-André Vincent*, Cahiers du dessin français, no. 4, Paris, 1987.

**Daniell 1825**
William Daniell, *A Voyage Round Great Britain, Undertaken in the Summer of the Year 1813, and Commencing from the Land's-End, Cornwall*, London, 1825, vol. 8.

**Delacroix 2001**
Eugène Delacroix, *Selected Letters, 1813–1863*, selected and translated by Jean Stewart, Boston, 2001, reprint of 1971 ed.

**Díaz Padrón 1995**
Matías Díaz Padrón, *El Siglo de Rubens en el Museo del Prado. Catálogo Razonado de Pintura Flamenca del Siglio XVII*, 2 vols., Madrid, 1995.

**Donop 1902**
Lionel von Donop, *Katalog der Handzeichnungen, Aquarelle und Ölstudien in der Königlichen Nationalgalerie*, Berlin, 1902.

**Elen 1995**
Albert J. Elen, "'Ongemeen uitvoerig op Perkament met sapverven behandeld': De gekleurde tekeningen van Willem van Mieris uit de collectie Jonas Witsen," *Delineavit et sculpsit* 15, 1995, pp. 1–22.

**Ford 1948**
Brinsely Ford, "The Dartmouth Collection of Drawings by Richard Wilson," *The Burlington Magazine* 90, no. 549 (December 1948), pp. 337–45.

**Ford 1951**
Brinsely Ford, *The Drawings of Richard Wilson*, London, 1951.

**Grote 1999**
Ludwig Grote, *Die Brüder Olivier und die deutsche Romantik*, Berlin, 1999.

**Hackert 1812**
Jacob Philipp Hackert, "Fragmente über die Landschaftsmalerei," in Johann Wolfgang von Goethe, *Hackert (Goethes Sämmtliche Schriften*, XVIII*)*, Vienna, 1812.

**Ingamells 1992**
John Ingamells, *The Wallace Collection Catalogue of Pictures, IV: Dutch and Flemish*, London, 1992.

**Kitson 1937**
Sydney D. Kitson, *The Life of John Sell Cotman*, London, 1937.

**Lister 1981**
Raymond Lister, *George Richmond: A Critical Biography*, London, 1981.

**Lister 1988**
Raymond Lister, *Catalogue Raisonné of the Works of Samuel Palmer*, Cambridge, 1988.

**Llewellyn 1996**
B. Llewellyn, "Roberts, David," in *The Dictionary of Art*, vol. 26, New York, 1996, pp. 463–64.

**Maherault 1880**
F. Maherault, *L'Oeuvre gravé de Jean-Michel Moreau le jeune*, 1880.

**Maselis et al. 1999**
Marie-Christiane Maselis, Arnout Balis, and Roger H. Marijnissen, *The Albums of Anselmus de Boodt (1550–1632): Natural History Painting at the Court of Rudolph II in Prague,* Tielt, Belgium, 1999.

**Matyjasczkiewicz and Llewellyn (forthcoming)**
Krystyna Matyjasczkiewicz and Briony Llewellyn, *David Roberts: Catalogue Raisonné* (forthcoming).

**Mitchell 1989**
Timothy F. Mitchell, "Johann Christian Reinhart and the Transformation of Heroic Landscape, 1790–1800," *The Art Bulletin* 71, no. 4 (December 1989), pp. 646–59.

**Nordhoff 1994**
Claudia Nordhoff, *Jakob Philipp Hackert, 1737–1807: Verzeichnis seiner Werke,* 2 vols., Berlin, 1994.

**Ormond 1973**
Richard Ormond, *Early Victorian Portraits,* 2 vols., 1973.

**Rawlinson 1908–13**
W. C. Rawlinson, *The Engraved Work of J. M. W. Turner, R.A.,* London, 1908–13.

**Roberts 1999**
D. Roberts, *Egypt and Nubia; The Holy Land* [1842–49], 3 vols., New York, 1999.

**Rosenberg and Prat 1996**
Pierre Rosenberg and Louis-Antoine Prat, *Antoine Watteau 1684–1721: Catalogue raisonné des dessins,* 3 vols., Milan, 1996.

**Roundell 1974**
James Roundell, *Thomas Shotter Boys, 1803–1874,* London, 1974.

**Rücker and Stearn 1982**
Elisabeth Rücker and William T. Stearn, *Maria Sibylla Merian in Surinam,* London, 1982, vol. 2 (commentary), facsimile ed. of Maria Sibylla Merian: *Metamorphosis insectorum Surinamensium* (Amsterdam, 1705), London, 1980.

**Russell 1991**
Francis Russell, *The Loyd Collection of Paintings, Drawings and Sculptures,* [England?], 1991.

**Schoch et al. 2001**
Rainer Schoch, Matthias Mende, and Anna Scherbaum, eds., *Albrecht Dürer, Das druckgraphische Werk, Band 1: Kupferstiche, Eisenradierungen und Kaltnadelblätter,* Munich, London, and New York, 2001.

**Shanes 1979**
Eric Shanes, *Turner's Picturesque Views in England and Wales 1825–1838,* London, 1979.

**Sloan 1986**
Kim Sloan, *Alexander and John Robert Cozens: The Poetry of Landscape,* New Haven and London, 1986.

**Solkin 1978**
David Solkin, "Some New Light on the Drawings of Richard Wilson," *Master Drawings* 16/4 [winter 1978], pp. 404–14.

**Sotheby's 1973**
*Catalogue of Seven Sketch-books by John Robert Cozens,* sale catalogue, introduction by A. Blunt, Sotheby's, London, 29 November 1973.

**Stainton 1985**
Lindsay Stainton, *Turner's Venice,* London, 1985.

**Sunderland 1970**
John Sunderland, "John Hamilton Mortimer and Salvator Rosa," *The Burlington Magazine* 112, no. 809 (August 1970), pp. 520–31.

**Sunderland 1988**
John Sunderland, "John Hamilton Mortimer: His Life and Works," *The Walpole Society,* vol. 52, 1988.

**Thuret 1711**
Jacques Thuret, *Oeuvres de Jean Berain, recueillies par les soins du Sieur Thuret,* Paris, 1711.

**Turner 2006**
Jane Shoaf Turner, *Dutch Drawings in The Pierpont Morgan Library, Seventeenth to Nineteenth Centuries,* 2 vols., New York, 2006.

**Vignau-Wilberg 1969**
Thea Vignau-Wilberg, *Die emblematische Elemente im Werke Joris Hoefnagels,* 2 vols., Leiden, 1969.

**Vignau-Wilberg 1994**
*Archetypa studiaque patris Georgii Hoefnagelii, 1592: Nature, Poetry and Science in Art Around 1600,* introduction by Thea Vignau-Wilberg, Munich, 1994.

**Watteau**
Antoine Watteau, *Figures de différents caractères, de paysages, & d'etudiez dessinées d'après nature . . . ,* Paris, [173–?].

**Weigert 1937**
R. A. Weigert, *Jean I Berain, dessinateur du chambre et du cabinet du roi (1640–1711),* Paris, 1937.

**Whistler 1948**
Laurence Whistler, *Rex Whistler: His Life and His Drawings,* London, 1948.

**Whistler 1960**
Laurence Whistler and Ronald Fuller, *The Work of Rex Whistler,* London, 1960.

**Whistler 1985**
Laurence Whistler, *The Laughter and the Urn: The Life of Rex Whistler,* London, 1985.

**Willsdon 2000**
Clare A. P. Willsdon, *Mural Painting in Britain 1840-1940: Image and Meaning,* New York, 2000.

**Wilton 1977**
Andrew Wilton, *British Watercolours 1750–1850,* Oxford, 1977.

**Wilton 1979**
Andrew Wilton, *J. M. W. Turner: His Art and Life,* New York, 1979.

**Wilton 1980**
Andrew Wilton, *The Art of Alexander and John Robert Cozens,* New Haven, 1980.

**Wilton-Ely 1994**
John Wilton-Ely, *Giovanni Battista Piranesi: The Complete Etchings,* vol. 1, San Francisco, 1994.


## EXHIBITIONS


**Aix-en-Provence 1954**
Musée des tapisseries, Aix-en-Provence, *Le Décor Berain,* catalogue by R. A. Weigert, 1954.

**Amsterdam 1972**
Gebr. Douwes Fine Art, Amsterdam, *Tentoonstelling van aquarellen uit europese landen van 1600 tot heden,* 1972.

**Amsterdam 1989**
Rijksmuseum, Amsterdam, *De verzameling van mr. Carel Vosmaer (1826–1888),* catalogue ed. by J. F. Heijbroek, 1989.

**Baltimore and elsewhere 1984–85**
Baltimore Museum of Art, Museum of Fine Arts, Boston, and Minneapolis Institute of Arts, *Regency to Empire: French Printmaking 1715–1814,* catalogue by Victor Carlson et al., 1984–85.

**Berlin 1905**
Königliche National-Galerie, Berlin, *Ausstellung von Werken Adolph von Menzels,* 1905.

**Birmingham 1948–49**
Museum and Art Gallery, Birmingham, *Exhibition of Pictures by Richard Wilson and His Circle,* 1948–49.

**Bristol and London 1988–89**
City of Bristol Museum and Art Gallery and Tate Gallery, London, *Francis Danby, 1793–1861,* catalogue by Francis Greenacre, 1988–89.

**Brussels 1957**
*Catalogue de la peinture ancienne, Musées royaux des Beaux-Arts de Belgique,* Brussels, 1957.

**Calais 1961**
Musée des Beaux-Arts, Calais, *L'Aquarelle romantique en France et en Angleterre,* 1961.

**Cambridge 1984**
Fitzwilliam Museum, Cambridge, *Prints and Drawings by Adolph Menzel: A Selection from the Collections of the Museums of West Berlin,* catalogue ed. by Lucius Griesbach, 1984.

**Cambridge 1984a**
Fitzwilliam Museum, Cambridge, *Samuel Palmer and "The Ancients,"* catalogue by Raymond Lister, 1984.

**Düsseldorf 1990**
C. G. Boerner Inc., Düsseldorf, *Von Caspar David Friedrich zu Adolph Menzel. Deutsche Künstler im 19. Jahrhundert,* 1990.

**Düsseldorf 1999**
C. G. Boerner Inc., Düsseldorf, *Goethe, Boerner, and the Artists of Their Time,* 1999.

**Düsseldorf and New York 1992**
C. G. Boerner Inc., Düsseldorf and New York, *Von Huber bis Heckel: Graphik und Zeichnungen (Neue Lagerliste Nr. 99 [1992]),* 1992.

**Eastbourne and London 1968**
Towner Art Gallery, Eastbourne, and Kenwood House, London, *John Hamilton Mortimer ARA, 1740–1779: Paintings, Drawings and Prints,* catalogue by Benedict Nicolson, 1968.

**Edinburgh 1979**
National Gallery of Scotland, Edinburgh, *English Watercolours and Other Drawings: The Helen Barlow Bequest,* 1979.

**Edinburgh 1999–2000**
National Gallery of Scotland, Edinburgh, *Turner and Sir Walter Scott,* catalogue by Katrina Thomson, 1999–2000.

**Haarlem 1998**
Teyler Museum, Haarlem, *Maria Sibylla Merian (1647–1717): Artist and Naturalist,* catalogue ed. by Kurt Wettengl, 1998.

**Kenwood and elsewhere 1985–86**
Iveagh Bequest, Kenwood, Whitworth Art Gallery, Manchester, and Musée cantonal des Beaux-Arts, Lausanne, *Images of the Grand Tour, Louis Ducros,* 1985–86.

**Leipzig 1990–91**
Museum der Bildenden Künste, Leipzig (for C. G. Boerner), *Von Schongauer bis Beckmann. Zeichnungen und Druckgraphik aus Fünfhundert Jahren,* 1990–91.

**London 1814**
New Gallery, London, *Catalogue of an Exhibition of a Selection of the Pictures and Drawings of Richard Westall, R.A.,* 1814.

**London 1894**
*Pictures Drawings and Sculpture Forming the Collection Sir John Pender GCM, MP, from 10 Arlington Street, SW & Foot's Bray Place, Kent,* London, privately printed, 1894.

**London 1937**
Thomas Agnew & Sons, Ltd., London, *Annual Exhibition of Watercolours and Drawings,* 1937.

**London 1949**
Tate Gallery, London, *Richard Wilson and His Circle,* 1949.

**London 1960**
Commonwealth Institute, London, *The Daniells in India 1786–1793,* 1960.

**London 1960a**
The Reid Gallery, London, *Summer Exhibition,* 1960.

**London 1960b**
Victoria & Albert Museum, London, *Rex Whistler 1905–1944: A Memorial Exhibition,* 1960.

**London 1971**
Victoria & Albert Museum, London, *The Sketching Society 1799–1851,* catalogue by Jean Hamilton, 1971.

**London 1974**
Spink & Sons, London, *Artist Adventurers in Eighteenth-Century India: Thomas and William Daniell,* 1974.

**London 1981**
Thomas Agnew & Sons Ltd., London, *Life and Landscape in Britain 1670 to 1870,* 1981.

**London 1982–83**
Tate Gallery, London, *Richard Wilson: The Landscape of Reaction,* catalogue by David H. Solkin, 1982–83.

**London 1983**
Sotheby's, London, 30 March 1983, lot 107.

**London 1984**
Victoria & Albert Museum, London, *Rococo: Art and Design in Hogarth's England,* catalogue ed. by Michael Snodin, 1984.

**London 1985**
Royal Academy of Arts, London, *Edward Lear, 1812–1888,* catalogue by Vivien Noakes, 1985.

**London 1986**
Barbican Art Gallery, London, *David Roberts,* catalogue by Helen Guiterman and Briony Llewellyn, 1986.

**London 1990**
Thomas Agnew & Sons Ltd., London, *English Watercolours and Drawings,* 1990.

**London 1996–97**
Royal Academy of Arts, London, *From Mantegna to Picasso: Drawings from the Thaw Collection at The Pierpont Morgan Library, New York,* catalogue by Cara Dufour Denison et al., 1996–97.

**London 2001**
Thomas Agnew & Sons Ltd., London, *Missing Pages: George Richmond R.A., 1809–1896, Drawings, Watercolours, Letters, Journals & Notebooks,* catalogue by Susan Sloman, 2001.

**London 2001a**
Thomas Agnew & Sons Ltd., London, *Watercolours and Drawings,* 2001.

**London 2002**
Thomas Agnew & Sons Ltd., London, *Watercolours and Drawings,* 2002.

**London 2006**
Tate Britain, London, *Gothic Nightmares: Fuseli, Blake and the Romantic Imagination,* catalogue by Martin Myrone, 2006.

**London and Manchester 2005**
Dulwich Picture Gallery, London, and Whitworth Art Gallery, Manchester, *The Triumph of Watercolour: The Early Years of the Royal Watercolour Society 1805–55,* catalogue by Tim Wilcox, 2005.

**London and New York 2005–6**
British Museum, London, and Metropolitan Museum of Art, New York, *Samuel Palmer, 1805–1881: Vision and Landscape*, catalogue by William Vaughan, Elizabeth E. Barker, and Colin Harrison, 2005–6.

**London and Rome 1996–97**
Tate Gallery, London, and Palazzo delle Esposizioni, Rome, *Grand Tour: The Lure of Italy in the Eighteenth Century*, catalogue ed. by Andrew Wilton and Ilaria Bignamini, 1996–97.

**London and Washington 1993**
Royal Academy of Arts, London, and National Gallery of Art, Washington, D.C., *The Great Age of British Watercolors 1750–1880*, catalogue by Andrew Wilton and Anne Lyles, 1993.

**London and elsewhere 1982–83**
Tate Gallery, London, National Museum of Wales, Cardiff, and Yale Center for British Art, New Haven, *Richard Wilson, The Language of Reaction*, catalogue by David H. Solkin, 1982–83.

**London and elsewhere 1982–83a**
Victoria & Albert Museum, London, Whitworth Art Gallery, Manchester, and City of Bristol Museum and Art Gallery, *John Sell Cotman 1782–1842*, catalogue by Miklos Rajna, 1982–83.

**Louisville 1977**
J. B. Speed Art Museum, Louisville, *British Watercolours: A Golden Age, 1750–1850*, 1977.

**Manchester 1937**
Whitworth Art Gallery, Manchester, *Exhibition of Water-colour Drawings by J. R. Cozens and J. S. Cotman*, 1937.

**Nancy 1961**
Musée des Beaux-Arts, Nancy, *Jean Berain (1640–1711): ornemaniste et dessinateur des menus plaisirs de Louis XIV*, 1961.

**Nancy 2004**
Musée Historique Lorrain, Nancy, *Stanislas; or, un roi de Pologne en Lorrain*, 2004.

**Newcastle-upon-Tyne 1953**
Laing Art Gallery, Newcastle-upon-Tyne, *Coronation Exhibitions*, 1953.

**New Haven 1985**
Yale Center for British Art, New Haven, *The Art of Paul Sandby*, catalogue ed. by Bruce Robertson, 1985.

**New Haven 2000**
Yale Center for British Art, New Haven, *Edward Lear and the Art of Travel*, catalogue by Scott Wilcox, 2000.

**New York 1988–89**
The Pierpont Morgan Library, New York, *The Romantic Spirit: German Drawings, 1780–1850, from the Nationalgalerie (Staatliche Museen, Berlin) and the Kupferstich-Kabinett (Staatliche Kunstsammlungen, Dresden), German Democratic Republic*, catalogue by Peter Betthausen et al., 1988–89.

**New York 1995**
W. M. Brady & Co., Inc., New York, *Old Master Drawings*, 1995.

**New York 1996**
C. G. Boerner, Inc., New York, *Selected Drawings*, 1996.

**New York 1996a**
The Pierpont Morgan Library, New York, *Fantasy and Reality: Drawings from the Sunny Crawford von Bülow Fund*, catalogue by Cara Denison, 1996.

**New York 1997**
Artemis Fine Arts Inc., New York, *Rome 1780–1790, Colored Views of Rome and the Campagna by Louis Ducros, Francesco Panini and Others*, 1997.

**New York 1997a**
The Pierpont Morgan Library, New York, *From Romanticism to Realism: German Drawings in The Pierpont Morgan Library*, 1997. No catalogue.

**New York 2000**
*The Morgan Library: An American Masterpiece*, New York, 2000.

**New York 2001–2**
Haboldt & Co., New York, *Northern European Old Master Drawings and Oil Sketches*, 2001–2.

**New York 2002**
The Pierpont Morgan Library, New York, *David to Cézanne: Nineteenth-Century French Drawings*, exhibition brochure by Cara Denison, 2002.

**New York 2003**
The Pierpont Morgan Library, New York, *Picturing Natural History: Flora and Fauna in Drawings, Manuscripts, and Printed Books*, exhibition brochure by Kathleen Stuart, 2003.

**New York 2003a**
C. G. Boerner, Inc., New York, *Master Drawings*, 2003.

**New York 2004**
Artemis-C. G. Boerner, New York, *Old Master Drawings & Paintings*, 2004.

**New York 2005**
W. M. Brady & Co., Inc., New York, *Master Drawings, Oil Sketches and Sculpture 1740–1900*, 2005.

**New York 2006**
The Pierpont Morgan Library, New York, *From Rembrandt to van Gogh: Dutch Drawings from the Morgan*, 2006. No catalogue.

**New York 2006a**
The Pierpont Morgan Library, New York, *From Leonardo to Pollock: Master Drawings from the Morgan Library*, catalogue by Rhoda Eitel-Porter et al., 2006.

**Nottingham and London 1974**
Nottingham University, Nottingham, and Thomas Agnew & Sons Ltd., London, *Thomas Shotter Boys Centenary Exhibition*, 1974.

**Paris 1994–95**
Institut du Monde Arabe, Paris, *Delacroix: le voyage au Maroc*, 1994–95.

**Paris and New York [1996]**
Didier Aaron, Inc., Paris and New York, *Catalogue IV*, [1996].

**Paris and elsewhere 1993**
Musée du Louvre, Paris, Museo Civico, Piacenza, and Herzog Anton Ulrich Museum, Braunschweig, *Giovanni Paolo Panini 1691–1765*, catalogue by Ferdinando Arisi, 1993.

**Paris and elsewhere 1996–97**
Musée d'Orsay, Paris, National Gallery of Art, Washington, D.C., and Alte Nationalgalerie, Berlin, *Adolph Menzel 1815–1905: Between Romanticism and Impressionism*, 1996–97.

**Philadelphia and Houston 2000**
Philadelphia Museum of Art and Museum of Fine Arts, Houston, *Art in Rome in the Eighteenth Century*, catalogue ed. by Edgar Peters Bowron and Joseph J. Rishel, 2000.

**San Marino 1986–87**
Henry E. Huntington Library and Art Gallery, San Marino, *British Landscape Watercolours from Southern Californian Collections*, 1986–87.

**Washington 1995**
Smithsonian Institution, Washington, D.C., *Voyages and Visions: Nineteenth-Century European Images of the Middle East from the Victoria and Albert Museum*, catalogue by E. Atil, C. Newton, and S. Searight, 1995.

# *Index of Artists*



# *Credits*

*Every effort has been made to trace copyright owners and photographers. The Morgan apologizes for any unintentional omissions and would be pleased in such cases to add an acknowledgment in future editions.*

PHOTOGRAPHIC COPYRIGHT

No. 9, fig. 1, Dépôt du Musée du château de Versailles © Musée Lorrain, Nancy; No. 24, fig. 1, Clore Collection, Tate Gallery, London/Art Resource, NY; No. 10, fig. 1, Collection Musée de Valence, dépôt du Musée du Louvre; No. 30, fig. 1, © Board of Trustees, National Gallery of Art, Washington, gift of Gaillard F. Ravenel and Frances P. Smyth-Ravenel, 2000.7.32. (PR); No. 35, fig. 1, Print Collection, Miriam and Ira D. Wallach Division of Art, Prints and Photographs, The New York Public Library, Astor, Lenox and Tilden Foundations; No. 18, fig. 1, The Whitworth Art Gallery, the University of Manchester.

PHOTOGRAPHY

Nos. 1, 3, Schecter Lee; No. 9, fig. 1, P. Mignot; No. 10, fig. 1, Philippe Petiot; Nos. 2, 4–37, Joseph Zehavi.